# COMEDY IN KHAKEE

## The Humorous Memoirs of a Policeman

**PRAKASH MISHRA**

An imprint of
Srishti Publishers & Distributors

**Srishti Publishers & Distributors**
A unit of AJR Publishing LLP
212A, Peacock Lane
Shahpur Jat, New Delhi – 110 049

editorial@srishtipublishers.com

First published by Bold,
an imprint of Srishti Publishers & Distributors in 2025



10 9 8 7 6 5 4 3 2

This is a work of non-fiction. All accounts narrated in this book are real-life accounts as experienced by the author. Though some events have been fictionalised for dramatic effect. The contents of the book are not intended to hurt any individual, community, religion, group, or institution and are purely for entertainment purpose.



Printed and bound in India.

*To my parents,*
*who gave me the gift of dreams*
*and the ability to realise them.*

# Praise for the Book

Khakee is usually serious business. There are challenging situations—dealing with criminals, facing riotous situations, regulating crowds, detecting cases, chasing robbers, facing bullets et al. And yet, as Prakash Mishra has shown in his book, *Comedy in Khakee,* there is a lot of humour also in uniform. One should have the right sense to see and enjoy it. His book is a delightful collage of hilarious incidents from his school days to his career in Khakee. It is finding happiness in the smallest incidents of everyday life, a celebration of humour, and an endorsement of the attitude to enjoy life as it comes.

—**Prakash Singh,**
*Former DG BSF, DGP UP and Assam*

In the often sombre world of policing, where gravity frequently eclipses life's lighter moments, *Comedy in Khakee* serves as a heartfelt reminder of the healing power of humour and the value of laughter. Prakash's compilation of anecdotes, reflections, and observations highlights some lighter side of policing and invites readers to relish something delightfully whimsical.

—**D. Sivanandhan,**
*Former Commissioner of Police, Mumbai and DGP, Maharashtra.*

In *Comedy in Khakee,* Prakash Mishra hilariously peels back the layers of policing to reveal its unexpected human side. From childhood pranks involving rubber rabbits and startled saints, school pranks that taught lessons in strategic planning, to police academy antics that blend grit and giggles, this memoir is a masterclass in finding humour amidst the chaos. Mishra's knack for turning tense situations into laugh-out-loud moments proves that even in 'Khakee', laughter is the best shield. Whether it's the struggles of a recruit with rogue horses or an innocent prank misfiring spectacularly, this book is a delightful reminder that the lighter side of life can illuminate even the sternest of callings. Prepare for a rollercoaster of laughter and life lessons served with a twinkle in the eye and a tug at the heartstrings.

—**Nitin Gokhale,**
*National Security Analyst, Senior Journalist and Author*

# Contents

# Acknowledgements

Creating *Comedy in Khakee* has been an incredible journey, one that I could not have embarked upon alone. There are many people whose support, encouragement and contributions have made this book possible, and I am deeply grateful to each of them.

After retiring from a highly stressful job, I realised that life is too short to be constantly wound up tighter than a clock in a watchmaker's shop. It was time to relax and merrily coast on the lazy river of existence. Writing was never on my agenda. I am, indeed, grateful to my wife, Sandhya, daughter Pallavi, elder brother Prasanna and my dear friends, Sanjeev and Thiagarajan, who took turns to shake me out of that overwhelming desire to lead the life of a sloth bear. I had to report to them every day as to how far I had progressed. My son, Varun, son-in-law Saurav, daughter-in-law Neha, and my twin brother, Pramode, also joined the group as the chapters progressed. But for their goading, this book would never have been completed. My granddaughter, Vidhi, who is shaping up to be a prolific reader, kept on asking me about the book and if she could read it. I simply could not let her down.

I am grateful to my friends, Tapan Patnaik, Sudhir Pillai and Sampad, for their inputs now and then, which helped me immensely in rounding corners.

A special thanks to my literary agent, Suhail Mathur and his enthusiastic group, The Book Bakers. Your guidance, expertise, and tireless efforts have been instrumental in bringing this book to life.

I am also grateful to Arup Bose and his team at Srishti Publishers & Distributors for believing in this project. Your unwavering support and dedication have been instrumental in sharing these stories with my literary audience.

Lastly, to all the readers who have picked up this book: Thank you for taking this journey with me. I hope these pages bring you as much joy and laughter as they brought me writing them.

With heartfelt thanks,
Prakash Mishra

# Preface

In an environment of policing, where seriousness often overshadows the joys of life, *Comedy in Khakee* seeks to remind us of the power of humour and the importance of laughter. This book is a collection of anecdotes, musings and observations that explore the lighter side of human existence. It is an invitation to step back from the daily grind and embrace the absurd, the ironic, and the whimsical.

Humour has always been a fundamental part of our lives, a universal language that transcends cultural and social boundaries. Through the lens of jest, we can examine the complexities of the human condition with a sense of detachment, allowing us to confront our fears, follies, and frustrations with a smile.

As you turn these pages, you will find tales that are both entertaining and thought-provoking. Some may make you laugh out loud, while others might evoke a knowing smile. Yet, beyond the laughter, there is a deeper message: that life, with all its unpredictability and chaos, is best navigated with a sense of humour.

This book is for all those who find joy in the little things, and who can see the funny side of life even in the darkest of times. It is for the jesters among us who remind us not to take ourselves too seriously and bring light into our lives with their wit and charm.

So, take a moment to relax, set aside your worries, and dive into a world where everything is *Comedy in Khakcc*. Lel these pages be a respite from the mundane, a celebration of humour and a tribute to the timeless art of laughter.

# In Pursuit of Happiness

*A day without laughter is a day wasted.*

—Charlie Chaplin

I did not know who Charlie Chaplin was when I was a child, but had somehow got hooked on this philosophy. I loved to laugh, even at silly things, much to the annoyance of others.

They often asked me, "What is there to laugh at in this?" How would they know? Laughter is so beautiful. It brings about happiness.

It all started very early in life in the company of my twin brother. Like all children, we used to play together and enjoy each other's company. There was no need to look elsewhere for a friend of our age.

Our father was posted as the district magistrate in a place called Sambalpur. We had a lovely two-storey house, where the first floor was the residence and the ground floor was used as a residential office. Lots of people visited the residential office for various kinds of work.

One day, we saw a man with a flowing beard making his way to the office. He appeared as someone who strongly adhered to the Gandhian way of life, both in attire and attitude. He even carried a spinning wheel with him. After having met my father, he decided to spend some time on the veranda outside and spin threads using his wheel.

This was something quite new to both of us. We did not know that he had stayed the night and had resumed his spinning since early morning. Both of us were playing on the first-floor veranda, throwing a toy rabbit made of rubber at each other. At some stage, my brother looked down and was quite intrigued to see the bearded man still sitting there, spinning with deep concentration.

Both of us had a quick discussion, and it was decided that the rabbit should be dropped down to see how the man reacted. The rabbit took a perfect vertical dive, landed on the spinning wheel, ricocheted off it, and then hit the ground.

Though there was not much of a sound, this sudden appearance of a rubber rabbit from thin air was enough to startle someone focused totally on the wheel and the slender thread. The man jumped up, letting out a howl, which sounded something like, "*Baap re baap!*"

It took him some time to comprehend the situation. After all, when a saintly person, deep in concentration and probably in close communion with God, is pelted with a rubber rabbit as an answer to his prayers, it is certainly a cause for serious introspection. He picked up the offending object gingerly and examined it closely.

Being satisfied that it would not cause any further damage or surprise him by exploding, he looked up, possibly to find out from where the rabbit had emerged. He saw both of us standing on the veranda, merrily grinning at having successfully accomplished our mission. He required no further evidence.

The pacifism associated with Gandhian philosophy was forgotten, and he started screaming and shouting, waving the rabbit at us. From the cacophony, we could somehow make out that he intended to complain about us to our father. We decided to leave the scene immediately. In the evening, our father came home, holding the rabbit in his hand and looking for both of us. We sheepishly appeared before him and were afraid to look at him. Our remorseful expressions perhaps melted his heart as he left without saying anything to us.

***

In school, the teachers often found me chuckling at something or the other. I do not know why it annoyed them so much, for they would make me stand on the bench, a very harsh punishment by any standard, but even that used to make me laugh. It was a rare opportunity to be at a height and look down on others.

There were many kinds of punishment in school, which, proceeding from the simple to the complicated, would go like this: standing up, standing up on the bench, kneeling down (near the blackboard), being sent out of the classroom and kneeling down outside the classroom. At times, when delinquency of a very grave nature was detected, even physical action was resorted to by way of hurling the duster at the delinquent.

Looking back, I am happy that I had never crossed the 'standing up on the bench' stage of delinquency. Others being punished was also a source of joy. Our friend, Sangram, would often be sent out of the classroom. Once, he decided to play a trick on the teacher. While he was standing outside, he asked the teacher, "May I come in, sir?"

The teacher looked a bit perplexed and said, "No."

After a minute, Sangram again asked, "May I come in, sir?"

The teacher said loudly, "No."

In response, Sangram coolly walked in and took his seat.

The teacher was shaking with rage. "What is this?" he shouted.

"Sir, you had told us that two negatives make a positive, so after the second 'no', I had to walk in."

Even the teacher was quite impressed with his logic and laughed. That was Sangram for you, showing sparks of his genius quite early in life. No one had ever imagined that he would be a pioneer in manufacturing fibreglass water tanks and boats in the country.

***

Each one of us was pursuing his mission to find happiness. For us, if school life had to be meaningful, playful pranks were a must. If one has not rolled a piece of paper into a thin straw and poked it surreptitiously into the ear of someone sitting next to him, he has missed so much. How could I miss out on this? I decided to plunge in and started looking for opportunities, which could be utilised to create interesting situations, leading to mirth and laughter.

Our history teacher was a strict disciplinarian. He would abruptly pick out someone in the class and ask him a question. Once, Rabi, who used to sit next to me, was keenly listening to the ongoing lecture on the Mughals. Whether he was actually listening or was lost in his own world was difficult to say. His past performance in answering these impromptu questions had been dismal. He used to stare at the teacher and then stammer out something, which was not even close to the answer. As a Good Samaritan, I had decided to help him, if necessary.

Rabi was again suddenly picked out by our history teacher. "Rabi, what were Akbar's achievements?"

Rabi stood up and stared at the teacher. Before he could say anything, I thought it was appropriate to come to his rescue.

The area around Bhubaneswar and Cuttack was not known for any industries. All it could boast of was a small ceramic factory and a Gudakhu factory. Gudakhu is a paste made by mixing lime, tobacco and molasses. The paste is rubbed over the teeth and gums to give one some kind of heady feeling. The people of our state and the neighbouring ones have a great love for this product. The factory was owned and run by one Akbar Khan.

I was ready with my help for Rabi. As he kept standing and staring at the teacher, I leaned towards him and said, "Sir, Akbar established a Gudakhu factory near Cuttack."

Rabi repeated my words.

The history teacher was absolutely stunned and furious. "Gudakhu factory? You said Gudakhu factory? Rabi! Stand up on the bench," he ordered.

Then he found me chuckling merrily. I was also ordered to stand up.

Rabi remained totally cold and non-responsive to me for about a week.

***

We had a dreaded lady teacher, Mrs V, who had the reputation of delivering slaps at the slightest hint of indiscipline. With the intention of ensuring that all students keep abreast with current affairs, she had scheduled a library period, during which we had to go through the newspapers. She would then come to the class and pick out anyone to tell her about some important news of the day. One day, I found Bijay in the library, frantically turning the pages of the newspapers.

"What is the matter, Bijay?"

"I cannot find any good news in the newspaper. What will I tell Mrs V?"

I gave him a concerned look and opened the newspaper. There was a big quarter-page advertisement for a cigarette named SCISSORS, with a picture of Biswajeet, a known actor of those days. The advertisement read – *Biswajeet says Scissors is a good cigarette.*

I showed it to Bijay and said, "Here it is – your good news for the day."

He looked a bit uncertain and asked, "Will this be good news?"

"Of course! Biswajeet is a renowned actor, and he is saying something. Isn't it news?"

He reluctantly agreed.

Bijay was picked out by Mrs V after about four or five others had been questioned.

"Bijay, what have you read today?"

He stood up confidently and spoke, "Madam, Biswajeet says that Scissors is a good cigarette."

He flashed a wide smile, thinking that he had done pretty well.

"What?" Mrs V's voice sounded like an explosion. "Shameless fellow! You are smiling?" She walked towards Bijay and gave him a tight slap. "Get out of the class!" she thundered.

Bijay went out of the classroom. He took about two weeks to become normal with me.

***

After these incidents, my efforts to help others did not meet with much success. Even the dumbest ones had somehow realised that I would only spell trouble for them. It was during this period of lull, when I was in serious contemplation to adopt new strategies, that something quite spectacular happened.

The first incident was related to our morning assembly. The new headmaster had introduced a minute of silence and self-contemplation after the procedures of the morning assembly were over. Everyone remained quiet with eyes closed for a minute and thereafter, we dispersed.

When you have a school assembly full of enthusiastic boys and girls, expecting them to close their eyes and remain silent is asking for a bit too much. Once the minute of silence started, someone would make a funny noise or intentionally cough or sneeze, followed by subdued giggles.

It required a lot of effort not to burst out laughing. One day, this exercise of disrupting the minute's silence was taken to an exceptionally higher level. As soon as silence was imposed, we heard a loud sound of a water cistern being pulled with great force repeatedly. The sound was coming from the first-floor toilet, located just above the place of assembly.

It made such a racket that even the headmaster was visibly rattled and shaken out of his meditation. This was repeated the next day as well. This time, the management was prepared. Our physical training teachers rose to the occasion and ran with great speed up the stairs.

Their valiant efforts, however, went in vain, as the desperados had charted their escape very cleverly. They ran down the other flight of stairs and merged with the students.

However, the physical training teachers were not ones to easily give up. After their dismal failure, they had to prove that they were better in strategy. The next morning, as soon as the racket started, the two of them took different stairs to rush upstairs.

The two miscreants were very predictable. They followed the same pattern for escape as they had successfully executed the previous day. As a result, when they were rushing down, using the second flight of stairs, they found, to their horror, one of the teachers rushing up. The mischief was successfully stopped. The episode was my first lesson on strategic planning. This school was turning out to be a good learning ground.

***

It was in this school that I learnt that rascals can be of different types. It so happened that we had gone to the canteen one day. It was not every day that we could afford the luxury of going to the canteen. Tiffin, carried from home, was usually our means to fight off hunger during the lunch break. There were occasions, too, when we felt like going to the canteen just to have some kind of outing.

That day, when we reached the canteen, we found our friend, Siladitya, already there. He was engaged in some kind of animated discussion with one of the canteen boys. There appeared to be some dispute over the delayed serving on the boy's part of an order for some item. The heated argument continued for some time.

At this stage, our English teacher, Mr Mishra, was seen coming into the canteen. He was a man of short height but had a sharp temperament. As he entered, the verbal duel between the canteen boy and Siladitya was taking a rather ugly turn. Siladitya had grabbed the canteen boy by the collar and appeared ready to become more aggressive when Mr Mishra shrieked.

"Ahhhh! What is going on?"

With these words, he rushed towards them and caught hold of Siladitya. It was beyond Mr Mishra's comprehension that a student who was expected to follow the noble path would go to this extent. "Siladitya! You are not a simple rascal but a dangerous one," rebuked the irate teacher.

There was a pin-drop silence. Gradually, everyone went about their ways. We learnt for the first time that there could be simple rascals and dangerous ones, too. Though I had a strong desire to ask for clarification on the identifying features of a simple rascal, I thought it was better not to disturb Mr Mishra. I could make out that he was in a heightened state of excitement, as evidenced by the way he was breathing. That was to be expected. After all, he had just dealt with a dangerous one.

***

While such exploits were happening in the school at fairly regular intervals, my pursuit outside the school, along with my brother, continued. Each day, there would be some prank or mischief, but an instance, which I can recollect with ease, happened when we were at home.

A distant relative named Dhruba from our father's village had desired to stay in our house temporarily. He occupied a small room on the flanks and spent most of his time in it. Both my brother and I used to visit him at times and indulge in small talk.

One day, in school, someone gave my brother a small nut kind of plant product with a very hard shell. He was told that if the nut is rubbed on the floor for some time, the shell becomes extremely hot. It was a new thing for both of us and had to be tested. A subject was required to see the effects of this experiment.

We went to Dhruba. He was happy to see us. As I engaged him in conversation, my brother got to work and started rubbing the nut on the floor. Dhruba was attired in a lungi and his lower thighs, just above the knees, were uncovered. After rubbing the nut for the recommended period, my brother touched Dhruba's thigh with it. What followed was simply unbelievable.

"Eeeeeiii!" Dhruba screamed and thrashed the affected leg in the air twice or thrice. Perhaps he was under the impression that he had been bitten by some dangerous insect and wanted to dislodge it from his thigh. It was at this stage that we committed the cardinal mistake of bursting out into uncontrollable laughter. Dhruba looked at both of us with such venom in his eyes that we decided to leave the scene immediately. Thereafter, Dhruba decided to end our friendly gossip sessions and turned sullen and suspicious of our every move. Both of us also decided to stay away from him.

***

We had heard of an incident involving our elder brother when he was in school. It had made waves in our family and was still recounted with a lot of enthusiasm.

Our father was posted in a distant district. To ensure that my elder brother got good schooling, it was decided to leave him with my uncle in Bhubaneswar.

My brother stayed with my uncle's family and pursued his studies. My uncle had a daughter who was also of the same age. Soon, my father's nephew also came from his village to stay with them and get a proper education. As there were three students in the house, it was decided that they should study together seriously.

My uncle's house was not very big. To dedicate a separate room for the studies of these three was simply out of the question, as there were smaller children, too, in the house. The neighbouring house was occupied by a gentleman who, being a bachelor, lived with his mother. He readily agreed to spare a room for the studies of these three students in the evening hours.

The academic pursuit of the determined students started in earnest. They used to go to the neighbour's house in the evening, study there for about two to three hours and then return home in time for dinner. This continued smoothly for a few days. My brother started getting a little irritated with my father's nephew, as he was slightly slow in everything. However, what really annoyed my brother was the fact that he used to take considerable time coming out of the room, even after study hours.

He had a habit of arranging his books, placing them properly, checking again to see if he had left everything in order, and then slowly walking out. This lengthy procedure detained my brother, who was eager to get back for dinner. He decided that the nephew had to be taught a lesson.

One evening, having finished his studies, my brother came out of the room and hid himself behind the door. It was dark outside, but he thought it was the best time to catch the nephew off guard. The wait was turning out to be agonising. Mr Nephew was taking an unusually long time to arrange his books.

Eventually, my brother detected some movement in the shadows emerging from the room. He prepared himself for the final assault. A person emerged from inside the room and as he crossed the door, my brother jumped out with a yell, or rather a bark, "Bho!"

The person reacted with a pathetic wail, "Aaaaaaaaaee!"

Then he started going around in a circle. When one faces any serious danger, it is quite in order for him to run away from the affected place as fast as possible, but this person, for some reason, opted to run in a circular motion, exposing him to greater risk. It was quite evident that the suddenness of the bark had startled him to such an extent that the portion of the brain responsible for logical thinking had been badly disturbed.

The matter grew more complicated when my brother, upon looking closely, found to his horror that the person going around in circles did not even slightly resemble Mr Nephew. A closer look revealed that he was the owner of the house, who had so graciously allowed them to use the room.

By this time, he had finished running his third circle. My brother decided to vanish from the scene. The matter was not revealed to anyone, but the next day, the mother of the victim complained to my aunt. She also informed that her son had contracted a high fever in the night and was quite delirious. The sharp bark had affected him terribly and had even impacted the functioning of the body's thermostat in the brain.

Profuse apologies on the part of my aunt and a guarantee that this kind of act will not be repeated in the future somehow saved the situation. The gracious gentleman recovered from the shock and showed no signs of any rancour or revenge, but for reasons of safety, never ventured to come out again for his quota of fresh air till the young students were in his home.

***

This incident had left a great impression on me and I was constantly looking for some occasion where I could put this great experiment to use. Our school days were over and we joined a college. The atmosphere there was certainly more liberating. Moreover, it was a meeting ground for students from different schools, each coming with his or her sub-culture.

The merger of all these varieties of people created a field for adventurous experimentation to an incredible extent and a demonstration of it took place sooner than expected.

We had a senior teacher who used to teach us Shakespearean plays. It was a class that had to be attended by all students, irrespective of their elective subjects. A big classroom was assigned to it. All the girl students used to sit at a right angle next to the podium and the boys were lined up in several rows in the front.

The English teacher, Mr Khan, was a senior man and behaved as if he could teach Shakespeare and his likes a thing or two. He would come to the classroom, pull his chair, swipe the table with the attendance register and then start his Shakespearean antics. What caused a lot of annoyance for most of the boys was his lecherous habit of trying to impress the girls by acting as though he was King Lear himself.

He failed to make much of an impact on any of the girls, but he kept at it. Some of the boys thought that enough was enough, and the man had to be brought to his senses. An elaborate plan was chalked out.

Diwali was around the corner and shops had started selling crackers. Among these were pistols for children, which used small red-coloured charges. When the pistol was pressed, there was a loud bang. Packets of these charges were available and could be used to produce sound if they were pressed against any hard surface.

The diabolical plan involved placing a few of these red-coloured round pistol charges under all four legs of the chair and table used by Mr Khan. The chair was pushed under the table so that it had to be pulled out if anyone wanted to use it.

The procedure was completed by a handful of conspirators before the other students came into the classroom. Soon, the entire class, including the girls, had assembled. Mr Khan made his dramatic entry, looked directly at the girls, flashed a big smile, proceeded to the rostrum and pulled out his chair. There were two loud bangs in quick succession.

Mr Khan took his hands off the chair instantly and jumped back. He kept looking at the chair for a few seconds. His smile had vanished, and I could see that his lips were quivering. He was, perhaps, waiting for something else to happen. When there was no further sound or movement, he thought that it was time to move on.

Not wanting to take any further chances with the chair, he approached the table from the front side and decided to sit on it. The moment he parked himself, there was a loud bang. Mr Khan was a bit on the heavier side and his weight was enough for the charges under the four legs of the table to go off in unison.

He jumped up like a frightened cat. This time, his whole body was shaking, and he was unable to contemplate his next move. The second explosion had opened up the possibility of more occurring if he made a wrong move. Now he had no place to sit. All he could do was to stand clear of the furniture and stare at it.

He could not even look at the girls for solace, as he did not want them to see his pitiable condition. It took him a minute or two to gather his wits. All the conspirators in this crime had occupied the front rows, as they wanted a ring-side view of the proceedings. Though mighty pleased with what had just happened, their faces displayed concern.

Mr Khan looked at them and spoke in a shaky voice, "This kind of thing should not happen in a class."

"It is very unfortunate, sir," someone replied.

"Yes. There are a lot of responsible boys here," he said, pointing at a few in the first row, mostly the perpetrators. "I entrust you with the responsibility of seeing that such incidents do not happen again."

That day, he was too disturbed to discuss Shakespeare. Instead, he delivered a passionate lecture on the subjects of good conduct and character building.

***

The system of proxy attendance was something that one learnt in college. Many a time, students would skip classes, but to ensure that their attendance was in order would request someone to say 'Present, Sir' when their roll number was called out. In a large class, this usually went unnoticed, and the lecturer marked the physically absent student as being present.

Nisith was one student who rarely attended classes and was on a perpetual request list for proxy attendance. One day, he made a rare appearance in the class to attend a lecture. He had no clue about what class he was attending and did not even remember his roll number.

Gagan, who had been his proxy attendee, thought it was a good time to teach Nisith a lesson.

He handed a number to him, saying that this was his and he should stand up and respond when it was called out. Nisith was very excited, as he was to personally mark his attendance for the first time. When the number was called out, Nisith stood up and responded loudly, "Present, sir."

He, as well as the lecturer, was taken aback when a girl also responded to the same number. The attendance marking is usually a smooth process and goes on without any halt or interruption. This was an unusual situation when two students and that too of different sexes responded to a roll number. The lecturer called the number again.

Nisith was not one to give up so easily. He stood up again and contested that it was his number. The girl also stood up. It was now up to the lecturer to resolve this delicate issue. He put down the register on the table and referred to the name written against the number. He read out the name of the girl. Nisith was unable to make out what had gone wrong. He looked around and found everyone chuckling.

"Sit down," he was ordered sternly by the lecturer. "You don't even know your roll number?"

Having no answer, Nisith gave up and sat down.

***

College life went on, providing many such hilarious occasions. While all this was going on, I always had a great desire to put the great experiment of my brother to use. I got one such opportunity when we were completing our post-graduation.

One of our friends had been selected to join the Air Force. He had organised a celebratory dinner party for quite a few of us. All of us assembled at his place at the appointed hour. I noticed some of the invitees gathering in a corner and speaking in hushed tones. News had been spreading through the campus that a few of them had been experimenting with some kind of drug available in the market.

This drug, it seems, had the effect of sending them to a world of ecstasy. I was sure that this group in the corner had already finished consuming it and were already on the path to the seventh heaven of delight, as some kind of beatitude had taken over them. They had become non-communicative with lesser mortals like us and just sat staring at the sky or some distant object.

If this was bliss, I would any day stay miles away from it. That day, unfortunately, instead of keeping clear of them, I decided to try out my brother's experiment on them. I saw three of them making a move to go outside. Immediately, I ran out and hid behind the door. As they emerged, I sprang out with a bark, "Bho!"

The three of them stopped. There was no pathetic wail from any of them. One of them turned around. I was happy, anticipating that he would start going around in circles, but he did no such thing. Instead, he looked at me and came closer. He caught hold of my neck and started pressing it.

"I have caught the animal," he said.

Nobody had ever told me that in that blissful state, human beings could appear to them as animals. The situation was getting extremely dangerous. I was lucky that there was not much of an impact of my bark on the other two. At the moment, they were calm in their state of trance, but there was always a possibility that the trance could break.

I did some quick thinking and screamed with all my might. Fortunately, help arrived sooner than I had expected. Some force had to be used to free my neck from that vice-like grip. The three of them were told to leave. I regretted my choice of subjects as my experiment had failed badly. Even worse was the fact that those blighters thought I was some animal. It had turned out to be a miserable evening for me.

***

After this disaster, I had no great desire to continue this experiment. It had to be put on hold, and other avenues had to be explored. Those were the days when life was quite laid back. There was no television, smartphone or malls, and students were content travelling by bus or cycle.

Motorcycles or scooters were rarely used by the younger generation. A bicycle was a prized possession, a luxury confined to a few. There were categories among bicycles, the most sought-after brand being Raleigh, of English pedigree. There were very few amongst us who had a Raleigh cycle.

Bibhuti, one of our classmates, appeared one day with a shining cycle. All of us rushed to see it. It was a Raleigh, its green colour giving it a more premium look. Bibhuti was a shy person, an introvert, who was passionately possessive of his cycle and did not like anybody even touching it.

He probably cared for his cycle more than himself. It was always spotlessly clean and shining. I thought it was time to do something about the cycle. Bibhuti used to park his cycle in a stand with a double lock and key. There was no question of breaking the locks and taking the cycle for a ride.

It was decided that the best way to take Bibhuti down a notch would be to hide his cycle at some place where it would be difficult for him to find it. After some deliberation, we decided to lift the cycle up a big tree and suspend it from one of the branches. The delicate operation was carried out with utmost precision and the cycle was placed on one of the branches.

To add effect, I wrote 'HELP' on a sheet of paper and stuck it onto the cycle. Thereafter, we went about our ways and did not bother to find out what had happened to Bibhuti. When I returned home in the evening, I found Bibhuti engaged in some kind of discussion with my twin brother. I hid myself as I was unsure of how Bibhuti would react to seeing me, but was able to hear their discussion.

Bibhuti, it appeared, had decided to visit our house to meet my father and complain about me. My brother was desperately trying to dissuade him. Their conversation went on for some time.

"He could have hidden my cycle somewhere, but taking it up a tree?" Bibhuti was on the verge of tears.

"Tree?" Even my brother was surprised at my innovative idea.

"Yes. He had put the cycle up in a tree."

"My God! How did you bring it down?"

"I had a terrible time bringing it down. I had to call some people for help."

"Was it damaged in any way?"

"No. Fortunately, there was none, but anything could have happened."

"I will scold him and tell him not to do this again."

"Again? Will he do it again?"

"No, he will not."

Bibhuti looked relieved. I thought it was time for me to reveal myself.

He looked at me with tearful eyes and asked tremulously, "Why did you do this?"

I flashed the most sheepish smile that I could manage.

"I will protect your cycle as if it were my own from now on," I assured him.

He kept looking at me dolefully and was in no mood to accept my assurances. The poor fellow felt extremely hurt. Luckily for me, he decided to leave without further insisting on meeting our father.

***

Many years later, while in service, I was nominated for a three-month-long training course in the United States. I reached the academy for training and was allotted a room, which I had to share with William Slack from the Santa Clara Police Department.

He was more known by his nickname, Bill. He was a very pleasant and affable person and much older than me. Tim and Howdy were in the adjacent room. The four of us shared a toilet. Both Tim and Howdy were almost my age. Bill, being senior in age, was the self-proclaimed leader of our group of four.

He used to wake us up in the morning, order us to do this and that, force us to go for a morning run even if we did not feel like it, enquire how we had fared in the periodic tests and the like. Despite all this, we liked him because he was very affectionate. He had a coffee maker and would make coffee for all four of us every morning.

The euphoria of being in the US was fading fast, and I was getting bored with the daily routine, that too in a foreign land. At times, it was exasperating to have Bill bossing us around. One fine morning, he lectured us on how things had to be done properly and at the right time. The previous evening, Bill had asked Tim to go to the laundry to get our clothes, but he had not done so.

Bill decided to go and get the clothes himself. After he left, I decided that it was time we had some fun. Whenever Bill went to the laundry, on his return, he would go straight to the wardrobe and put the clothes away neatly. He was a very methodical man.

I called Tim and Howdy and discussed my plan to scare Bill that morning. They agreed to it immediately.

"Old Bill has started nagging us a lot," said Tim.

The plan was that I would hide inside the wardrobe and, as soon as Bill opened it, jump out. Tim and Howdy worked as lookouts. One was closely watching the corridor for Bill to return, while the other was to help me get inside the wardrobe and then close the door from outside.

Bill had left in a huff that morning while he was still in the process of brushing his teeth. So, all the while, he had the toothbrush inside his mouth. Soon, he was seen coming back with the clothes and the toothbrush sticking out of his mouth. We swung into action. I got inside the wardrobe and Howdy closed it. I was in total darkness. Straining my ears, I could hear some movement and then the wardrobe door opened. As soon as I saw Bill's face, I shouted, "HO!"

Bill was probably unable to shriek because of the toothbrush in his mouth, but his eyes opened wide in disbelief. He sprang back away from the wardrobe towards the bed. At this stage, I jumped out. As soon as I did so, he sprang back again, looked at me, and jumped back for the third time. With this jump, he fell back on the bed. He was breathing heavily and still staring at me.

"You could have killed me," he said. "I was about to swallow the toothbrush."

Both Tim and Howdy had vanished from the scene, but I could hear them chuckling. Thereafter, whenever Bill introduced me to someone, he would invariably say, "He looks innocent, but he jumps out of wardrobes."

***

Reminiscing the past, I am reminded of two incidents, which confirmed that my daughter and son had also picked up the right threads. One evening, I was standing with my five-year-old daughter on the veranda of our home in Cuttack. It was growing dark. We were on a ground-floor flat and the small veranda was open on two sides to an unkempt garden, which was a good playground for all types of stray dogs.

I was telling her a story, which she possibly did not find very interesting. Suddenly, I heard a growl, which sent a chill down my spine. I thought that a wild dog had entered the garden and could jump on the veranda at any time. Concerned for my little daughter, I caught hold of her and rushed inside.

"What happened?" she asked.

"There is some wild dog outside. We should get inside the house."

She went into a fit of laughter.

"Why are you laughing? Did you make that sound?"

"I scared you, didn't I?"

"Yes, you scared me well."

***

My son, younger than my daughter by five years, was not far behind. He was about four years old when we went to Calcutta. We were returning to Cuttack by train and had booked seats in a chair car. It was a long six-hour journey and obviously, the young boy was getting restless. He decided to introduce some spice into the journey.

There was a middle-aged person in the seat in front of us. The chair car had those pushback seats in which the back could be adjusted by a lever jutting out at the side. When the man dozed off, my son got up and pulled that lever. The backrest fell back with a jerk, and the poor man jumped up, shaken from his sleep.

The man was too embarrassed to initiate a probe into this mischief but preferred to remain awake and alert for the rest of the journey. He was convinced that someone had pulled the lever of his seat.

***

My heart swelled with pride the day my granddaughter jumped out from behind the door as I was coming into the house. I pretended to be shocked and shaken and she was absolutely thrilled. Having found in me a good mentor in her pursuit of happiness, one day, she came to me for help to play a prank on my niece.

We built a contraption, using a bangle, a rubber band and a coin folded in a sheet of paper. When one opened that packet, the coin twisted in the rubber band and started rotating and hitting against the paper, making a sound. Having succeeded in her mission of scaring my niece, my granddaughter ran back to me, looking mighty pleased.

Life becomes much better when one starts enjoying these small pleasures. Why should we surrender to the dull, drab and regular routine and lead a life without mirth and laughter? The child within us is waiting to be indulged. Let us not disappoint him.

# Rise and Grind

Plutarch, the famous Greek philosopher and historian who lived from 46 AD to 122 AD, said, "The mind is not a vessel to be filled but a fire to be kindled." Now, do not jump to any conclusions. I am neither trying to prove my scholastic abilities nor am I trying to impress people with such quotes. In fact, there is a background to it.

I received a call from a friend who sounded decidedly shell-shocked. He had some unexpected news to convey to me.

"I just heard that you have been selected for the IPS. Is that correct?"

I did not have the faintest clue, though I had actually appeared for the examination and even faced the interview.

"I don't know," I blurted out.

"Oh! If you have not heard, it must be wrong news." He sounded very pleased.

Such was my reputation. Not many people had any great hopes for my abilities. In fact, this far-from-flattering diagnosis of my capabilities had started quite early for me. With a fair amount of pain in my heart, I confess that once, our history teacher in school had, before the whole class, announced with strong conviction that he had no hopes for me.

I agree that in an independent country with freedom of speech, one is entitled to one's own opinion, but this public announcement had rather badly jolted my otherwise cheerful personality.

Anyway, this call from my so-called friend generated in me a strong desire to find out if the results had been declared and whether I had cleared the examination. Things are simpler now, but in 1977, one had to make great efforts to get information. There was no technology associated with information.

After making all sorts of enquiries, I finally learnt that a copy of the result was available with the local *Press Trust of India*. With a lot of apprehension in my mind, I called the PTI office and received confirmation that what my friend had heard was indeed true. I had made it. I was ecstatic. The past was forgotten; I had a future to look forward to.

I decided to become serious and take some remedial measures. I had never left the secure confines of my home, having received my entire education in Bhubaneswar. The prospect of moving out and brushing shoulders with others from more sophisticated backgrounds was haunting me.

I could ill afford to carry my old reputation along with me. So, off I dashed to a nearby library to search for something that I could use as a guiding beacon. If someone were to ask me, 'What is the purpose of your life?' or 'What do you think training can do for you?', I needed to have an impressive answer.

Good old Plutarch came to my rescue. His quote about the vessel and fire was perfect and seemed an answer to all future questions. My research and scholastic pursuits were rather short, but I was very pleased with the result. No more filling of the vessel; I had to now get down to the serious business of kindling the fire.

Soon, I received a letter, asking me to report for training in Hyderabad after a short stint in Nagpur. The National Civil Defence College was located in Nagpur, and we were to be instructed in various areas of civil defence and first aid. The stay at Nagpur provided an opportunity to break the ice with others who had come from different parts of the country.

It was quite an affable group, though it was too short a period to get to know everyone. The training was interesting and mostly uneventful, except for one typographical error that caused a lot of hilarity. Mrinal, a very serious officer who always introduced himself as M.K. Das, got the shock of his life when during attendance in one of the classes, the name 'U.K. Das' was called out.

"Sir, there is no U.K. Das here."

"Oh! It is a strange name. It says Urinal Kanti Das."

All of us burst out laughing. Mrinal's name had been misspelt; the 'M' had been replaced by 'U'. Poor Mrinal! To this day, he carries his new name, as we lovingly refer to him as Urinal Kanti Das.

***

From Nagpur, all of us, including Urinal Kanti, set sail for our ultimate goal – our would-be alma mater, the National Police Academy in Hyderabad. The ambience of the campus with its uniformed staff, the discipline and the crisp orders left us awestruck. Most of us had no idea of what the training would entail, though we had heard very disturbing tales of the tough outdoor and the more dangerous riding classes.

The first few days were quite relaxed, but once we received our uniforms and the customary haircut, things suddenly changed. Apart from IPS trainees, the batch had officers from the Nagaland and Sikkim Police. All combined, we were a group of a hundred and twenty trainees. For indoor classes, we were divided into two sections and for outdoor ones, into six squads.

The division into squads heralded the beginning of our misery. Being a member of a squad meant the start of regimentation. One's spirit, which had been wandering so happily till then without any concern for consequences, was now subjected to orders that had to be followed to the letter. Any deviation not only invited wrath and venom but physical retribution. What a mess I had got myself into!

Having dealt with such situations with every batch, the academy had well-planned strategies to harness the soaring spirit of every new entrant. The first in the chain of strategies was sleep deprivation. The wake-up call was at 4.30 in the morning, followed by getting ready at top speed, with a proper shave and then rushing to the ground to be in time for the fall in.

This was something that was totally unacceptable. After all, 4.30 a.m. is the time to have the best dreams. Being pulled out of bed at that time amounted to pure sadism. To be able to comply with such sadistic orders, one had to be equipped with some alarm mechanism. Unfortunately, I did not even have an alarm clock and had to depend on my country cousin, Praful, for the same.

Poor Praful's room was close to mine and once his sleep was shattered by his clock, he would waddle up to my room and let loose his pent-up anger on my door, banging it furiously. I would open the door, and we would exchange resigned, melancholic looks.

We would then get ready and rush downstairs to meet others passing through different stages of depressive melancholia. In the company of other tortured souls, the depression would gradually start to recede and by the time we reached the ground for the fall in, it would be gone. We were now ready to face the second onslaught.

The second in the chain of strategies was to subject the spirit to physical torture. We had to carry out various physical movements on the commands of the instructor who had perhaps never been exposed to the dangers of noise pollution. The commands were sharp barks, reaching ever-increasing decibel levels.

Each of the instructors would try to out-decibel the others and you could clearly see the glee on their faces after they had achieved the desired level. They had no concern for the poor souls, who were left gasping at such imperious misuse of lung power.

A couple of hours of such activities, which included marching, jumping, rope-climbing, running and anything else you can imagine under the sun to torture the so far carefully nurtured body, had the effect of breaking down all resistance, and by the time we were dismissed to return to the mess, each one of us was like a zombie.

Battered and bruised, both physically and mentally, we would enter the dining hall where the sight of a good breakfast would infuse us with some life and enthusiasm. Breakfast time was one of fun and frolic, with all of us happily eating and joking with each other. Soon, we encountered a new danger even in the dining hall.

It happened to be one from amongst us. Satyavrat Trivedi was a specimen. That he could qualify to call himself a human being was a wonder. His behaviour at the dining table could easily be classified as a grave danger to humanity. People were generally hungry after two hours of heavy physical activity, but Trivedi exhibited such a strong attachment to food that anyone coming in his way could meet with disastrous consequences.

One had heard of a disease called bulimia, which is an eating disorder. However, people afflicted with this disease are benign and eat without troubling others. Satyavrat was perhaps suffering from a different strain of this disease. He exhibited the signs and aggressiveness of a bulldog with bulimia.

Most of us soon realised that it was developing into a form of grave danger. He would snatch bowls of sugar, jam, butter and whatever else he set his sights on. Anyone near him would get scratched and pushed and though it did not happen, had a fair chance of getting bitten. It was then decided, purely from considerations of safety, to allow the bulldog with bulimia to occupy an entire table where he could eat to his heart's content, get up with a loud belch and walk away.

***

After breakfast and a quick bath, we were ready for classes. There was nothing very inspiring about the classes. They just reminded us of our college days, except for one difference. Here, one could see a lot of trainees in different *mudras* of sleep. After a tiring morning, the monotonous lectures sounded more like a lullaby to many sleep-deprived souls. Our lives had been transformed into the outdoor and the indoor classes. I kept wondering whether I had made the right decision. Where was the spark to kindle the fire?

It was then that I decided to take charge of the situation. A prophetic statement made by the previously referred to history teacher came floating to my mind. To appreciate the gravity of that prophetic statement, I would like to briefly narrate the circumstances under which it was made.

Our classroom was located in a corner, at the end of a corridor, next to the chemistry laboratory. The students of the science stream of our class would, to impress girls of our humanities stream, barge into our room at times, holding strange concoctions in test tubes. Sometimes, these concoctions would emit gases, sometimes bubbles and at times, change colour with the addition of more liquids.

One day, just before the history class, they entered the room with something which was emitting the most horrendous smell. The shrieks and gasps of the girls encouraged those science ruffians to come up with more potent versions of the same concoction. To make our lives miserable, they poured portions of the liquid at various places in the classroom and vanished.

As a result, our classroom started smelling as though thousands of dead rats were dumped in it. It was at this stage that the history teacher walked in. He was, I would say, quite badly affected. We had never seen him make such strange faces. He twisted his nose at different angles, perhaps under the misconception that there was something wrong with his olfactory senses. However, when the pungent smell continued despite his best efforts to reset his nose, he gave up, took a deep breath and sternly looked at me.

"What is all this?" he asked.

I narrated the sequence of events leading to this most smelly affair. On hearing about the chemistry laboratory, he rather reluctantly decided that I could not be behind this prank. He again took a deep breath, looked at the whole class and said, "What cannot be cured must be endured."

I had not pondered over the purport of this prophetic statement then, but at the present juncture, when life was becoming unbearable, the significance of these great words struck me as the work of an absolute genius. The agony had to be endured, but how?

Our history teacher had been exposed to the smell for a few minutes, but there was a torturous situation that promised to last for months. I had to make my own changes and adaptations to the great quote. With some serious thinking, I finally arrived at a satisfactory solution. The great quote was amended to read as:

"What cannot be cured must be endured with a smile."

That was it! I had to endure it with a smile. I soon found that in order to keep yourself amused, you had to look at small things, which could appear very insignificant from the point of view of training but would provide you with a lot of fun and mirth. It was basically the art of observing how some trainees responded or reacted when they faced conditions that they would have never imagined before.

I agree that it is highly improper to laugh at others' misery, but it was not the misery of others that I was looking for. I only intended to concentrate on different forms of human behaviour under stress. The first such attempt at this great behavioural study was made in an outdoor class.

Our batch was large and quite diverse. We had trainees from all regions and different backgrounds, who, most interestingly, ranged from very young to almost middle-aged. Some were very serious and some, extremely casual. Quite a few looked overawed by the situation and some behaved as if it was nothing.

Our squads had an even dispersal of characters of all types. The elderly ones looked somewhat flummoxed by the torture in the outdoor classes and were trying to come to terms with the physical onslaught. We had in our squad, one Pravesh, who was close to thirty and looked extremely serious, confused and eager to come to grips with the unfolding terror.

I decided to make him the first subject of my behavioural study. For a successful study, I thought that some input from my side would be in order. When we fell in the morning in three rows, I placed myself behind Pravesh with a handful of small pebbles in my closed fist. Pravesh was all concentration, expecting the sharp bark from our squad-in-charge and ready to respond to the command with all seriousness.

At this critical stage, I hit him behind his head with a pebble. He tried to look back, but the compulsion to look straight ahead made his mission of investigating the source of this missile a bit difficult. He gave up. It was then that I hit him with a second and third pebble in quick succession.

To say that he was perturbed would be a gross understatement. I could see his jaws drop, not once, but quite a few times. By then, the squad-in-charge had started barking his commands. Poor Pravesh had to stop even this movement of the jaw, which probably was giving him some solace in the difficult situation in which he found himself.

I suspended my release of further missiles and had to take an active part in the drill. However, I resumed my activities the next day. The result was similar. This continued for about a week. I could see that Pravesh was looking quite miserable. The unsolved mystery was clearly affecting him.

One day, I thought of bringing some variation into this experiment. I threw a small pebble at him when we were marching. This baffled him. He could not control himself and looked all around. In the process, he went out of step and was thoroughly admonished.

He was more sullen and despondent than ever before. Finally, one day, I was a bit reckless. I threw a pebble at him with gay abandon when our outdoor classes were over and we were going out of the parade ground. As I was completing the motion, Pravesh, for some mysterious reason, looked back and saw me.

“Oh!” was all he said.

I responded with a much feebler, “Oh!”

Thereafter, there was complete silence on both sides for a few seconds. I was apprehensive that he would call our squad-in-charge and lodge a formal complaint. Instead, strangely, he smiled broadly and came towards me. My apprehension increased, and I wondered if he would indulge in physical violence. I was preparing to defend myself when he reached me and enveloped me in a tight, friendly embrace.

"So, Prakashji, it was you," he said, releasing me. I grinned sheepishly in reply. "It is good that I saw you today. I was so worried about this."

"Why?" I queried.

"Why? You are asking me why? If you have pebbles falling on you without knowing the source, do you know what types of evil thoughts come to your mind?"

"Evil thoughts?"

"Yes. I thought it could be the work of some ghost or evil spirit."

"Oh!"

"Yes. Today, I am so happy. You know, outdoor classes also need a lot of concentration. I will now be able to give them my complete attention. You should also pay proper attention to the commands," he ended with this advice.

I agreed. The matter was satisfactorily resolved. I was touched by Pravesh's humility and grace. We became very good friends. Our friendship grew as the days passed.

The outdoor classes became more complex. There was something called a squad drill, where one had to twist and turn a squad into various formations. We were warned that in the examination, one would be asked to command the squad into very difficult formations. We never had the courage to ask as to why one should follow such complicated commands rather than politely asking the squad to come and stand in a particular order. This would be faster and with very little use of lung power. However, there were several such rational issues, which only remained as questions that were never asked.

Finally, the dreaded examination was scheduled. The test in squad drill was to be conducted before a panel of senior police officers who had been called from various places. Each one of us was to report before this body and the officers would give us a problem to be solved. The squad comprised constables from the CRPF, but four of us, by rotation, manned the four corners of the squad as guides.

I was manning the right corner as the 'right guide' when Pravesh was summoned for the test. He reported before the panel and was given his problem of taking the squad and halting it at a right angle from its present location. What he understood was difficult for me to comprehend, but he came towards us and stood looking totally bewildered. I had heard the problem given to him and tried to extend some help.

One could not talk, so I had to take recourse to sign language. Even sign language had to be used under very restrictive conditions. The panel of eminent examiners was staring directly at us. All I could manage to do was turn the fingers of my left palm to the left. I thought it was a clear enough sign for Pravesh to command the squad to turn left.

Strangely, he remained quiet, looked at me and started moving his jaws as he did when those pebbles had hit him. The examiners were getting restive and shouted from behind. I started signalling more desperately for Pravesh to understand the intent. What was going through his mind was extremely difficult to comprehend, but I had a nasty feeling that perhaps, he was under the impression that I was back to my old pranks. His next move more or less confirmed my suspicion, as he banished me from his view.

He commanded, "*Piche mud!*"

We turned backwards. Now, all visual communication with him had ended. Next, he commanded, "*Tej chal!*"

We started marching away from him, waiting for his next command. However, no further orders came. We kept on marching and reached the edge of the parade ground. Not knowing what to do, we jumped over the small dividing brick wall and entered an area full of thorny bushes.

We kept on marching. Finally, our squad-in-charge came running from behind and ordered us to return. When we reached back, we found that Pravesh had been dismissed from the scene. His squad drill examination had ended under very unfortunate circumstances as he was given no marks for the same. He had to later repeat the test.

***

Outdoor classes encompassed a variety of activities. One such activity had to do with the functions of a guard. A guard normally comprised five to nine persons, depending on the role assigned to it. Each person had a different role to play. Our classes on guards were taken by our squad-in-charge, Teja Singh.

He was a tall and well-built man, having an imposing personality and a booming voice. He meticulously briefed us on how a guard commander should perform, how the entire guard should react in an emergency and so on. One day, he was briefing us on the role of a sentry.

"The sentry is supposed to challenge anyone who comes near after evening hours," he thundered. "He should not spare anybody, not even an officer who comes to check the guard."

"Then how is the person challenged supposed to respond?" one of us asked.

"If it is a common man, he should say '*dost*', but if he is an officer who has come to check the guard, he has to respond by saying 'round'. Now, I will give you a demonstration of how the sentry is to challenge any such person. Narayan *Saab*, you become the round officer."

I do not know why he picked Narayan. Narayan was a quiet and gentle soul who took his classes seriously. Being from Tamil Nadu, he was not very proficient in Hindi but managed everything extremely well. Everyone liked him. All of us were ready for the upcoming demonstration. Teja Singh took his position as a sentry with a rifle by his side, the metal bayonet glistening in the morning sun.

Narayan was asked to march to some distance, take a reverse turn and come towards the sentry. He marched away in great style and after quite some distance, turned back and started his march towards the sentry. He was about twenty to thirty steps away when suddenly, Teja Singh leapt up in the air.

While airborne, he could accomplish quite a few things with extreme ease. His left foot lunged forward, the rifle with the glistening bayonet changed from a vertical to a horizontal position and in his thundering voice, he shouted, "*Tham! Kaun ata hai?*"

His landing and conclusion of the loud challenge coincided with absolute precision. The huge leap had taken him quite close to Narayan. Our attention was now on Narayan. On seeing this strange spectacle and hearing the loud challenge, he froze. There was complete silence for a few seconds.

Teja Singh was looking at Narayan with his bayonet pointing straight towards him. Narayan was perhaps thinking that these were the last moments of his life. He could only muster enough strength to meekly say, "*Dost.*"

"You should say 'round' not '*dost*'. I had asked you to be the round officer."

After being thus admonished, Narayan returned to our file, thoroughly shaken.

***

Incidents like these kept me quite amused and interested in the outdoor classes. There were several incidents in the riding ground, too. Each day brought a new episode, and we all got used to it. The most disastrous episode that forms part of the equestrian folklore is the incident when a trainee was thrown off his horse and after he had fallen down, the horse, for some reason, kicked him in the abdomen, resulting in serious internal injuries, leading to his tragic death.

This incident affected not only every trainee for years to come but also their parents. My father had reminded me of this incident when I was to join the service, pleading with me to be extremely careful with horses. There were incidents where a horse would suddenly gallop away from the riding ground with the poor fellow on top and take him all around the nearby areas.

I had heard of an incident involving an officer from my state who had had a miserable experience while riding during his training. His horse had suddenly broken off from the pack and galloped away towards Naki Lake, a tourist attraction in Mt. Abu, where the academy was located in those days.

The horse ran around the lake with such speed that the poor fellow's hat was blown off. He was completely at the horse's mercy. Thankfully, after a few rounds, the horse decided to return. This had happened with other trainees, too. Some, however, did not have the good fortune of completing the entire trip, as they were thrown off the saddle and had to walk or limp back.

Even after the academy shifted to Hyderabad, the horses, once in a while, decided to break out on such trips planned entirely by them. As there was no lake nearby, they would gallop along the railway track located close by and then decide to return. There were many incidents of people falling off them.

There were reported incidents of the trainee suddenly getting unseated from the saddle as the horse bucked, landing him on the neck of the horse. With this background information, I decided to be careful as instructed by my father. Soon, incidents started happening to us, too.

A new and complicated dimension was added to this saga of horror even before we had mounted a horse. Our first exposure to horses was when we were taught to saddle and bridle them. This involved standing near the horse, assembling the saddle and bridle and then carefully placing them on it.

One morning, when this exercise was on, Brar, our dear friend, screamed. The scream rattled all of us, including the instructors. Brar revealed that while he was busy putting the saddle on the back of his horse, the other horse standing near him bit him. That horses can bite too raised our apprehensions to new levels.

Once proper riding started, we observed the misery of some who were thrown off and some who never dared to even move their horses. They kept on sitting and staring at others. I had my first experience of a fall when we were going on a cross-country ride along with a few others.

While returning, we ran into a pack of sheep and goats who were out for grazing. One of the horses from our group suddenly bolted and ran into a field filled with water. The poor rider landed in the water, while the horse came out of it. Thereafter, the other horses also picked up on this idea of fun and started behaving as if they were the masters.

Even our instructor, who was accompanying us, was not spared. Our hearts sank when he could not manage to stay in the saddle and fell to the ground. My horse, Girnar, one of the youngest in the group, took a particular fancy to a small goat kid. The kid, who was merrily running around, would suddenly stop, turn back, jump and run again.

This intrigued Girnar. He observed the kid for a considerable time and then decided to imitate his actions without any consideration for me. He started running, stopped suddenly and then turned back. At this stage, he saw the kid jump up on all fours and while in the air, attempt a turning manoeuvre.

This caught the fancy of Girnar and he decided that it was time to dislodge me. If he were to attempt such acrobatic moves, the dead weight on his back had to be thrown off. He bucked so suddenly that I had no chance of holding on. I landed at a safe distance from him and watched him jump up in glee and run towards that kid. The training staff somehow managed to control the horses, and I was made to mount Girnar again. The remaining part of the ride was completed without incident.

***

Indoor classes were not as eventful. Except for the fact that almost every day, someone or the other had to be woken up from deep slumber, there was not much action in them. There were two sets of instructors for our indoor classes. The majority were police officers in uniform and a few who taught us subjects like forensic science, forensic medicine, law and Hindi were non-uniformed.

One could be more relaxed in the classes taken by the non-uniformed faculty as they were quite informal. Our Hindi teacher, Mr Pandey, was perhaps under the impression that we did not take him seriously. He used to constantly remind us that he was also the controller of examinations and that all our papers and examination results were kept in an almirah in his room.

However, the threat of the almirah did not deter many of us from playing some pranks in his class. Hindi classes were not mandatory for all of us. They were primarily for trainees who came from non-Hindi-speaking states. Hence, while the others were enjoying a good nap after lunch, we unfortunate souls had to report to the Hindi class.

Our pent-up anger and frustration were released by letting off some funny sounds or calls when Mr Pandey would be busy writing on the blackboard. Mr Pandey, being a seasoned campaigner and having taught many batches of non-Hindi-speaking blokes, took such incidents with a pinch of salt. However, one incident really shook him to the core.

We had a trainee from Nagaland named Ngulie. Like all Nagas, he was full of life and energy. He loved to do whatever pleased him, without bothering about the consequences. If he felt like pulling someone's hair, he would do it without batting an eyelid. I simply adored him for this quality.

If Ngulie was around, there was bound to be some interesting activity. Ngulie was also with us in the non-Hindi-speaking group and attended the Hindi classes. One day, he came to class wearing his breeches. He had his riding class immediately after the Hindi one. For some strange reason, Ngulie, who loved sitting in the back benches, occupied the front row.

Mr Pandey was lecturing on how to communicate in Hindi. At times, he would turn towards the blackboard and write some words. Ngulie was watching the proceedings silently. Our eyes were on the blackboard as Mr Pandey was writing something. Suddenly, there was the sound of a thump followed by a short yelp.

I found that Ngulie was in a crouching position behind Mr Pandey. The thump was the effect of Ngulie jumping and the yelp had emanated from Mr Pandey, who was visibly startled by the sound, while he was still focused on writing on the blackboard.

Mr Pandey turned back to see what had happened and on seeing the situation, he yelped even louder. He must have found the situation quite intimidating. The sight of Ngulie, in breeches and in a crouching position, close to his posterior, affected him very strongly.

Breeches are fine if one is on horseback, but on *terra firma*, they give one a totally different look – that of an old-time warrior or the like. A Naga in breeches in a crouching position must have sent shivers down Mr Pandey's spine. He was breathing heavily and his face had turned as red as a turnip. When he managed to regain his breath, he blurted out, "What is this?"

He spoke in English. The Hindi teacher perhaps thought that, in a crisis, English would have a better admonishing effect. By this time, Ngulie had given up his crouching position and was standing upright. In fact, Mr Pandey's second and louder yelp had the effect of not only sending him back a few steps but also putting him in a state of remorse. He was no longer his usual exuberant self.

"I was practising '*ghode ke samne baith* (sitting before the horse)'," he replied.

'*Ghode ke samne baith*' is a command given in our saddling and bridling class. On this command, we are supposed to leap forward into a crouching position and start assembling the saddle and bridle and thereafter, put them on the horses standing before us. Ngulie, it seems, had his saddling and bridling examination after the Hindi class and therefore, thought that he could do a practice session in the Hindi class itself.

"You think I am a horse?" Mr Pandey shouted back.

Having regained his breath and the colour of his face, Mr Pandey was in no mood to give up. We had to intervene and explain to him about the impending examination and how important it was to finish the task in time. Being the controller of examinations, he realised the importance of the matter and asked Ngulie to return to his seat.

***

Soon, the days and months passed by and we reached the end of this difficult training. The adverse situations that we first encountered became very bearable as we decided not to get overtly affected by them. Rather, looking for occasions, which were available in plenty, to make one laugh and enjoy made my task much easier.

It was the first spark that I found to kindle the fire, a spark which reminds me always that no problem is insurmountable. With a cool mind and without getting rattled by adverse situations, one can really achieve a lot. Plutarch was right.

# Shikar

I was tearing my hair out, trying to make sense of a wretched register called Khatian. I had been told by very wise people that if one masters the art of writing and interpreting a Khatian, one has mastered the art of police station management. The process of mastering was suddenly interrupted when Mr Swain, the officer-in-charge, came into the room.

"Sir, will you be interested in joining us for *shikar* tonight?"

I had reported at Keonjhar a few weeks ago, in July 1979, to undergo my district training as an assistant superintendent of police (under training). The words 'under training', enclosed in brackets, were magical. They brought you close to almost everyone in the police fraternity. They gave you enormous love and affection without much responsibility. Since I did not throw my weight around or flash my ego, each and every one of them wanted to give me as much input as possible so that they could take pride in contributing to the building of an officer.

Keonjhar is, or rather was, a small sleepy town those days with a population of a few thousand. The district was large, rich in mineral resources and had wonderful forests and hills. Recent years have seen a transformation in the economy as well as the culture of the entire area with mining activities, both legal and illegal, reaching proportions that no one had ever imagined. People, in general, were simple, law-abiding and contented. The roads were almost empty with very few vehicles. One could cycle around happily, especially while doing night rounds along with other police officers. The police had very few vehicles. The SP had a car and apart from that, there were just a couple of Jeeps.

The SP, Mr Nayak, was a fine person. He was very affectionate and caring. He gave me complete freedom to do things on my own and report to him on a weekly basis. After a few days in his office, I was attached to an urban police station. Since the SP wanted to monitor my progress, he preferred that I be attached to the Keonjhar police station. The officer-in-charge was Mr Swain, an experienced officer who taught me everything that one had to learn about the running of a police station. He was a cheerful and extremely resourceful man, full of energy and zest.

The police station also housed the office of the circle inspector of police. The circle inspector supervised the functioning of about six police stations in his circle. Mr Mohanty, the circle inspector, was a man of medium height and had a somewhat ungainly figure. His lower legs were normal, but he exhibited a distinct ballooning effect from his knees upwards right up to the neck. The overall effect of all the oversized parts made him look like a full circle and completely justified his designation of the circle inspector.

I soon realised that his looks were quite deceptive. He was, at one time, a famous football player and also good at badminton. There was an open-air badminton court in the police station premises. Mr Mohanty once insisted that I play against him. Badminton was never my game, but I agreed as I felt that it would be quite easy to take him on. As the game progressed, he performed some incredible drop shots. He could flick his wrist to perfection and the shuttle would behave exactly as he wanted. I turned out to be a total mismatch for him.

My daily routine started with a visit to the police lines to attend the parade and interact with the men. The reserve inspector or the sergeant major, Mr Banerjee, was a lean and handsome man who had earned the reputation of being a good marksman. After the police lines, I would spend the rest of the day at the police station. Mr Swain used to take me along for investigations, spot visits and examination of witnesses. At the police station, I was exposed to writing case diaries and the maintenance of other records. Both Mr Swain and Mr Mohanty took a lot of interest in mentoring me.

Once, I had excitedly mentioned to them our riding classes in the academy during training and how we used to enjoy them. To my surprise, the next evening, I saw a small horse in the police station premises.

"Whose horse is this?" I asked Swain.

"Sir, we got this so that we can do some riding, too."

"Great! But don't you think it's a bit too short?"

"It will be okay for us, Sir."

He mounted the horse and took a round of the campus.

Soon, Mohanty, the inspector, came out and wanted to take his turn at riding. With much difficulty, he mounted the horse, but the poor little animal, not accustomed to such a heavy load, refused to move. Swain tried his best to drag the horse but in vain. Finally, Mohanty gave up and had to dismount. He gave a piece of his mind to Swain for acquiring such a useless animal. The next day, neither did I find the horse around nor were any questions asked.

The invitation to join the *shikar* was music to my ears. It immediately transported me to the days of the Raj, the exploits of Jim Corbett and other stories, some real and many imaginary, which various 'spirited' officers had boasted of during mess nights at Cuttack. I had to experience it myself. The invitation had to be grabbed, and I did so with both hands.

"Do we have to inform the SP about it?"

"No, Sir. We will be away just for a few hours. He will not know about it. Moreover, we are going on a night round only."

Mr Mohanty had, by then, joined our conversation. He was also of the same view. I felt reassured and asked, "Who are the others joining us?"

"Sir, we will ask Banerjee to join us. He is a good shot. We have also asked Laltoo to accompany us."

"Who is Laltoo?"

"Sir, he is a relative of the Raja of Keonjhar and a good *shikari*."

"Can we take Mr Kanungo along?"

Mr Kanungo had come to Keonjhar to set up a new sponge iron plant. He was earlier in Bhilai and had much experience in *shikar*. He owned a few rifles and was always on the lookout for a trip to the jungles.

"Sure, Sir."

The composition of the team was complete. We had to now take care of the logistics. Arms and ammunition were available in plenty. Mr Kanungo had his rifles. Laltoo had a 12-bore gun and Banerjee was to bring a .303 rifle. An open jeep is always the preferred means of transport for such an excursion or at least, that is what I was given to understand. Mr Mohanty had an official jeep, which he used for touring different police stations. It was one of those old Willys models with a short chassis. It was petrol-driven. Mr Mohanty loved to drive it himself. Everything seemed fine with the jeep but for its brakes. A strange noise emanated as and when Mr Mohanty's heavy legs pressed the brake pedal. The vehicle would stop but only after a 'Cheeeeeen' sound.

With everything in place, we were to start after an early dinner. The group assembled at the police station and a final count of men and materials was done:

Arms? Ok.

Ammunition? Ok.

Lights? Ok.

With all systems set, we climbed into the vehicle. The hood had been removed, and the jeep looked battle-ready. The placement of men inside the jeep had to be based on a well-calculated strategy. Mr Mohanty was the driver. Mr Kanungo occupied the left front seat with his rifles by his side to cover the left flank. Banerjee, the ace marksman, was in the rear along with Laltoo and Swain. Swain was given the task of holding the focus light. I was placed in the front seat between the driver and Mr Kanungo. As a rookie, I was not expected to contribute but only witness and observe. It was not a very enviable situation; however, I was happy to be there.

So, off we started towards the hills and forests of Kanjipani. Kanjipani is a good 30 kilometres from Keonjhar, up a small hill. The area had good forests and once you left the main road, there were arterial roads branching off to the interior. A drive in a hoodless jeep has its own merits. A fine breeze kept blowing against us and with the moon and stars gazing down, there could be no better setting. The ride on the highway was quite smooth and fast and almost eventless. Not that anyone expected something on that stretch, but being a total novice, I was wondering if something might happen early.

It was time for us to leave the main road and turn left onto country roads. Soon after we turned, Mr Mohanty stopped the jeep. Swain jumped out, lifted the bonnet and fixed the wires of the spotlight. With the same speed and precision, he jumped back to his original position. We started moving again.

As the jungle grew denser, everyone became silent. It was time for serious concentration, though I was wondering what to concentrate on. Swain was moving the spotlight to the left and right, scanning the jungles for any signs of movement. Wild, terrifying thoughts came into my mind. The wonderful stories of the Raj faded away.

I was reminded of a story my uncle used to tell me when I was in school about a *shikar* where everything went wrong. He was a doctor and had worked during the British rule. There were a couple of English doctors working with him. One day, they received information that an inspection team of senior doctors were to visit from England. It was supposed to be a great event and apart from the excitement, there was a lot of nervousness all around. After all, it was not every day that one played host to such dignitaries.

There was even more nervousness and concern when one of the English doctors revealed that he had received instructions that the high-level inspecting party would love to go for a *shikar*. It was not to be an ordinary *shikar* but one whose sole purpose was to bag a royal Bengal tiger. This group of doctors was extremely peace-loving and had never had the slightest inclination or desire to harm even the smallest of animals. Thus, the prospect of organising this rather horrific event was quite depressing for them, but no one wanted to displease the important visitors.

Fortunately, one of the Indian doctors came forward and said that he knew people whom he could contact to satisfactorily address this issue. The experts were contacted, and they agreed to put everything in place.

The inspecting team arrived and was apprised of the arrangements. The date and time for the *shikar* was fixed in consultation with the experts. It was decided that one of the local doctors should accompany the team as a liaison man. The automatic choice was the one who had contacted the experts. Most reluctantly, he agreed, even though he did not have the faintest clue about *shikar* or for that matter, even what a jungle looked like.

The team assembled in the dead of night and proceeded to the appointed place. They soon reached the spot and saw a machan built for them on a tree. They managed to climb up with all their arms, ammunition and lighting equipment. The prime space on the machan was occupied by the Britishers who, for operational reasons, had to have a wide free area around them to have a proper arc of fire. This technicality being settled, very little space was left for the poor Indian doctor who had to place himself almost on the edge of the machan. Looking down, he saw a goat tied to a peg. It was bait, supposedly to lure the tiger to the spot.

Everyone settled down and waited quietly for the tiger to appear. The experts had guaranteed that a tiger was on the prowl in that area and the bait would certainly draw him to the spot. The Indian doctor had not contended with the combined effect of the cold night, the presence of such senior English doctors and the intimidating atmosphere of the jungle. He was shivering and maybe praying to get back early.

The intensity of his shivering increased further when he looked down at the poor goat. By then, the party had become used to the darkness and eerie silence. Suddenly, there was a sound of rustling leaves followed by a sharp bleat of the goat. Our Indian doctor, on the edge of the machan and in a state of shiver, had not seen anything like this before. The appearance of the tiger from nowhere pushed him into a state of extreme anxiety.

At this stage, the hunters switched on their lights to have a proper view before taking a shot. This startled the Indian doctor to such an extent that he forgot that he was on the edge. The poor fellow, terrified and shaking uncontrollably, fell off the machan.

It was now the tiger's turn to be startled. The sound of the falling doctor surprised the tiger, and he looked back. On seeing another prey, he left the goat and came menacingly towards the doctor. The great hunters on the machan were in a quandary over this sudden development. The doctor's sudden appearance near the tiger was never part of the plan; nor had they any indication that this local doctor had the will or inclination to engage a huge tiger in unarmed combat.

The doctor's desperate cries for help from below confirmed that his going down was not by intent but by a sad accident. The hunting expedition had, in a flash, turned into a rescue mission. The hunters decided to shoot the tiger in the head so that it would be killed instantaneously, thereby saving the doctor. When they looked down, they found that the tiger's head was dangerously close to that of the doctor. Even the sharpest of the shooters thought it was too risky to try a headshot as the situation below was becoming very complex.

Sometimes, the tiger's head was on top and suddenly, with a cry, the doctor's head would be above. A sense of panic was starting to engulf the hunters. In this state, they had no choice but to fire randomly just to scare the tiger away. Their persistent firing, the resultant sound and the pitiable screams of the doctor forced the tiger to flee the scene. The tiger's exit brought some relief, and the team climbed down from the machan. The doctor, badly mauled, was thus rescued, and the team retreated as fast as they could. I had not been able to find out from my uncle as to how the inspection proceeded after this disaster.

I was now in a more or less similar situation as the Indian doctor, seriously examining the prospect of some wild animal suddenly springing out of the darkness and entering our vehicle. I tried to comfort myself by rationalising that in case such a catastrophe did happen, the animal in question, if he had reasonable intelligence, would attack either the person on my right or left because of the large quantity of food that he would get. He would be a fool to pick a skinny fellow like me. That being said, who can predict what is reasonable or unreasonable for an animal when it is difficult to do so in the case of human beings?

I was struggling with these dark thoughts when Swain said, "Shhh." It was a warning, well-interpreted by Mohanty, who braked the vehicle with a 'Cheeeeeen'. No words were exchanged. The spotlight wandered on the right for some time and then fixed on a spot. There was a barking deer standing there, transfixed by the light and rooted to the spot.

Banerjee rose from his seat in the rear, a 12-bore in his hands. Mohanty was holding his breath. I didn't know why and it was not the time to ask either. Banerjee aimed and fired. There was a sound of a click but no bang. Everyone looked at Banerjee. Possibly, there was some exchange of coded messages through a movement of eyebrows, which I was unable to decode. Banerjee regained his composure and aimed with the second barrel and fired. Again, there was a click. A loud hiss, like a high-pressure hosepipe suddenly developing a leak, startled me. I looked towards the origin of the sound and found that it came from Mohanty. He had been holding his breath for too long and with two failures, he had to let it go along with his frustration. The barking deer remained there for a few more seconds and then jumped away into the darkness.

With the deer having disappeared, the temporary embargo on free speech was lifted. Everyone pounced on Banerjee. "How can you have two misfires?"

The dejected sergeant major opened the gun and looked into the breech. It was empty. The gun had never been loaded. Banerjee sat down, holding his head in his hands, a picture of woe. An opportunity had been lost. Banerjee was reprimanded for his carelessness. I am sure strong expletives would have been used, but my presence acted as a hindrance. Anyway, everyone soon calmed down and without any further bad blood, the team members pledged to be more professional in their approach.

We continued our pursuit. The second phase of the expedition was getting longer than anticipated. Everyone was losing patience and once again, Banerjee was subjected to a barrage of insults, including accusations that he had spoilt the entire trip, his presence was unlucky and so on and so forth. With the pent-up frustration being released, everyone relapsed into a gloomy silence.

Mohanty drove on. Finally, he announced that he would drive up on a diversion for about a kilometre after which the expedition would be called off. By then, I had also lost all interest in the *shikar* and the initial excitement was dead and gone. My mind had wandered to the prospect of resuming my struggle with the Khatian register the next day. The dull thought and the cool air made me doze off, and I woke up with a start, hearing a shrill 'Cheeeeeeen'. The jeep had stopped. The spotlight was fixed on some point about two hundred metres away. We all disembarked and looked keenly to see a group of wild boars moving.

The excitement that was dead and gone returned in abundance. Banerjee had alighted with his rifle and announced that it was loaded. The target was at a great distance, but Banerjee had his reputation at stake. He took the perfect position, aimed and fired. This time, there was a loud bang followed by a grunt from the target site. Everyone jumped in unison. One of the boars had been hit. Banerjee's past folly was forgotten. He got a pat on the back. The other boars ran away, while the one hit, moved in a circle and then fell on the ground.

Before I could realise what was happening, Swain handed me the spotlight. I kept it focused on the boar. Everyone started walking towards the spot, leaving me near the jeep with the light in my hands. It took quite some time for them to reach the spot. I was unable to hear what they were saying or discussing. They stood at a distance from the fallen boar and I saw Laltoo fire two rounds at it from his 12-bore. Nothing happened after that. They stood still for more than a minute, watching the boar.

Then they slowly converged on the prize kill. To me, they appeared like mime artists, performing with gestures. I could not hear anything they were saying. The mime artists, having converged on the kill, kept on performing, what seemed to me, quite meaningless motions of bending down and standing. This continued for some time. Finally, all of them bent down and picked up the boar together, each holding one of its legs. The fifth mime artist was possibly directing their movements.

They started walking back towards the jeep. They had hardly covered ten to fifteen steps when, all of a sudden, they dropped the boar on the ground and all five of them scampered off in different directions. Mohanty was running towards the jeep at full steam. He could have given any good sprinter a run for his money. Despite his bulk, he managed to run at an unbelievable speed with full determination. What had generated this sudden desire in all of them to take to sprinting was beyond my comprehension. I wondered if the instinct of self-preservation was behind this sudden burst of athletic activity.

As I was enjoying the lithe movements of Mohanty, who had by now reached the home stretch, I heard a kind of growl from behind me. It sounded something like a 'G' followed by several 'Rs'. I am not adept at identifying animals by the sounds they emanate, but I had an uncanny feeling that this particular combination of 'G' and 'Rs' was bad. It certainly did not sound like any herbivorous creature.

I felt a chill run down my spine, thinking that some ferocious creature was on its way. The grim prospect of a sizeable part of my posterior getting chewed off seemed real. The instinct of self-preservation that had apparently propelled Mohanty and others to such high speed took over me as well. I turned back with the light and started closely examining the area behind me. I could not see anything, but further examination was cut short as I heard an agonising cry of 'Ahhhh', followed by a frantic shout of 'Light, light!'

When I turned around and focussed the light towards the running track, I saw a terrible spectacle before me. Mohanty's final dash had had a disastrous end. Running on an undulated surface by itself is quite a difficult task. When the path that was clearly visible suddenly becomes dark, the sprinter's problems are compounded. Mohanty must have encountered severe navigational issues in the dark. The ultimate result was a crash landing. Fortunately for him, the crash site was a piece of land that had been tilled recently. Hence, the consequences of the unfortunate crash were not so severe. After the supply of adequate light was restored, he got up and started running again. He was determined to finish his sprint in time and style.

He reached the jeep in no time and climbed into his seat. Panting heavily, he gulped down some water from his bottle kept near the seat. He continued to pant heavily for some time. In a short span, his huge body had been deprived of all the elements so essential for the sustenance of life—light, air and water. I could imagine what he must have gone through. Soon, his breathing slowed down and became more rhythmic. It was time for debriefing.

"What happened?"

"You should never trust that rascal, Banerjee."

"What did Banerjee do?"

"What did he do? He said that the boar was dead."

"Wasn't the boar dead?"

"No! It wiggled its ears when we were carrying it."

"Wiggled its ears? Is it dangerous when a wounded boar wiggles its ears?"

He gave me a look of surprise because he was unable to comprehend that I could be so ignorant.

"Dangerous?" He volunteered to explain. "A wounded boar can be extremely dangerous. It can even kill an elephant!"

"Elephant?"

"Yes, an elephant."

Several questions were racing through my mind. Certainly, a boar might be dangerous if you irritate him by twisting his tail or pulling his whiskers (do boars have whiskers?), but I could not understand how having been grievously injured by a .303 bullet, it could prove to be a danger to an elephant unless it was powered by some nuclear device. This was not the time to debate on these technical issues. However, one thing appeared certain. Mohanty and the others must have had some first-hand experience of being chased by a boar at an impressionable stage of their lives. That must have been the reason for clocking such high speeds.

"Why did you turn the light away?" It was his turn to ask me.

"Oh! I heard the sound of an animal from behind me."

"Animal?"

"Yes." I repeated the sound of 'G' and 'Rs' to him.

"What? Are you sure?" He got down from the jeep with a look of disbelief. Maybe he wanted to start another sprint, but before he could do so, I assured him that I had seen no animal. He sat down again, but there was still a look of concern on his face. The events of the night, especially the sudden wiggling of the ears by an animal presumed dead, had completely unnerved him.

Further discourse on the capacity and destructive capabilities of an injured wild boar could not continue as we heard several gunshots in quick succession. The other four, who had run off in different directions, had re-converged for the final act of mime. This time, they were taking no chances. Like a demolition squad, they kept on firing at the boar on the ground. Satisfied that no parts were showing any signs of movement, they picked up their kill and started their journey back to the jeep. Soon, they arrived with the prize. There was a loud thud when they dropped the dead boar in the back of the jeep. It was not only huge but quite smelly.

"Chahh! It is stinking!" I shouted.

"What is stinking?"

"The boar."

"Boar? Wake up." It was my wife. "Were you dreaming of a boar?"

I woke up with a start. Had I been dreaming?

"Get up and get ready. You will be late for the parade."

I left for the parade and then for the police station. Everyone went about their tasks in a normal way. I sat down with the Khatian and looked at the entries intently, but my mind was elsewhere.

Had I actually gone for a *shikar*?

# Baptism by Fire

"Hari Om! Hari Om!"

Ambika *Babu,* the deputy superintendent of police in the office of SP Bhubaneswar kept on repeating these words, followed by some other chanting. He was extremely tense at the thought of our appointment with the DGP, who had given us time to meet him at Bhubaneswar in the SP's office. We had completed our district training and the three of us had sought an appointment with the DGP before we were given our first charge.

The anxiety and apprehension of Ambika *Babu* seemed to be quite well-founded. The DGP was known to belong to the very strict, no-nonsense variety of officers. Hence, Ambika *Babu* could really not come to terms with the fact that we had, of our own volition, decided to meet him. Ambika *Babu* had been assigned the task of receiving the DGP and also producing us before him.

"You are all new to the service. Learn to avoid superior officers as much as possible. Hari Om! Hari Om!"

His behaviour, which appeared quite melodramatic at the first instance, started affecting all three of us. We looked at each other with concern in our eyes. I was quietly wondering whether we had done the right thing in seeking this appointment. All of a sudden, my thoughts were interrupted by a loud shrill, "Oh Lord, save us!"

Jolted out of my thoughts, I looked around and discovered that this cry had emanated from Ambika *Babu*. What had made him change over to this appeal for mercy before the Lord from his usual 'Hari Om' baffled me. The answer was soon clear. Ambika *Babu* was staring fixedly at the main gate of the campus through which the DG's car was entering.

Ambika *Babu* sprang up from his chair, took a deep breath and with amazing speed, rushed out of the room. We heard the car come in, followed by the sound of the car door opening and closing. After that, there was hardly any sound, and we were left to wonder what was happening.

Even at this stage, I had a strong urge to abandon the whole thing and quietly slip away but realised that it was too late. After about ten minutes, the suspenseful period ended with the appearance of Ambika *Babu*.

"He will meet you now. Please follow me."

It was our turn to jump up. Quietly, we followed Ambika *Babu*. I could almost hear my heart beating loudly. Having reached close to the room where the DGP was sitting, we were asked to stop and wait to be shown in. Ambika *Babu* went inside. Soon, he came out and marched us into the room. We lined up in front of the DG and saluted him. He did not look at us and was busy going through some papers.

Finally, the silence ended with his asking, "So?"

It takes time to decipher such cryptic questions, but after some quick thinking, I managed to blurt out, "Sir, we have finished our district training. We are waiting for our first postings."

He looked at me for a second, glanced down and said, "You think you know everything about policing?"

Some further quick thinking prompted me to realise that this question should be best left unanswered. With no response from our side, he finally decided to give us his full attention.

"Okay. You will get your postings soon, but mind you, they will be very difficult places. You have to prove yourselves."

We were dismissed. Ambika *Babu* marched us out of the room. His final 'Hari Om' was one of relief. We came out, stunned, not knowing what the DGP meant by a 'difficult' posting.

Within a week, we got our orders. I was posted as ASP, City, Cuttack.

I had not the faintest idea that Cuttack would be a cesspool of misery. It happened to be the state police headquarters. It was the place where the DGP and other senior officers in the police hierarchy not only held office but also stayed. This meant that I had a more than fair chance of bumping into one of them at any time.

You could well imagine what my life had become, as I had to be in a state of readiness to face, what may be described in tactical language, as an ambush at any moment.

Soon, I found out that the senior group comprised three different characters. There were many others who were inherently good. They genuinely liked a young officer shaping up his life and career and did their best to not only mentor but also help in any possible way. A few could be described as grumpy, who pulled long faces if they felt that you did not measure up to their high standards of etiquette and conduct. There were a minuscule few who were outright uncouth and arrogant.

My immediate boss, the SP, was someone who could not be placed in any of these categories. He seemed to me someone who was under an illusion that he was God's gift, if not to mankind, at least to the police. He had memorised some common phrases like 'putting my foot down' or 'calling a spade a spade' and used them rather generously.

Whether he was totally ignorant of the meaning of these phrases or used them only for effect was very difficult to say, but he had never displayed any such conduct wherein his foot had left an impressive mark for others to follow.

After attending a few meetings of officers conducted by him, I realised that he was one of those who strongly believed that the use of obscenities and abuses was the best way of conveying to your subordinates that you were in full command and control.

Hence, he would regale us with vulgar words describing the human anatomy. Having done so, he would look mighty pleased with himself and display his pleasure by sucking in air from one corner of his mouth, a gesture, which, I am sure, he must have picked up in his formative years watching Hindi films, where a villain does something similar while watching a vamp's dance.

He never took a liking to me. He always looked at me as though I was some creep who would never fit into his scheme of things. The reason behind this could have been two-fold.

First, I had replaced an officer who was possibly very close to him and understood his needs properly. My sudden posting came as a big jolt to him and must have disrupted his well-set pattern. The second reason was that he perceived me as a threat. Since I had been posted at the instance of the DGP, he believed that I had been set as someone to spy on his activities. Little did he know that spying was never my forte, nor was I someone who would carry tales.

Anyway, there was little I could do to clear the air. All this, however, put me in a very difficult situation. It was my first posting and without the goodwill of the SP, I had to really struggle during it.

The whole state was witnessing a student agitation, which started in western Orissa. There used to be rallies and processions almost every day. One day, the students decided to demonstrate in front of the commissioner's office. Trouble was expected to brew and a police arrangement was chalked out.

The SP positioned himself in the collector's office, the Additional SP near the High Court and I was to be at the commissioner's office with a few officers and men. This meant that I was to be at the centre of trouble, while the more experienced seniors were to park themselves at places where no problem was anticipated.

Anyway, that was the scheme and I could not do much about it. I always had a strong conviction that a great leader had to lead from the front, but the time had now come to learn newer concepts in management – that of 'pushing from behind'. For a moment, I had a fleeting thought that maybe the SP wanted me to learn to take on greater responsibilities.

I was wondering about this possibility when we started hearing the slogans of the students coming from a distance. All our officers and men took positions as planned earlier. The gate of the office was locked with a large posse of policemen standing behind it.

Very soon, the procession of students, numbering around a thousand, reached the gate. There was heavy sloganeering followed by a lull. They were waiting for their leaders to deliver some inspirational speeches before launching the final assault.

At this stage, while I was standing with a couple of officers and watching the proceedings, I saw someone in plain clothes coming towards me. He came quite close and in a very low tone, whispered near my ear, "Saar?"

"Who are you?" I countered.

"District intelligence," he whispered back.

"Oh!"

"Yes," he confirmed.

His identity having been established, I asked him, "What do you want?"

"Situation report."

"What situation?"

"SP wants to know what the situation is."

"Can't you see?"

"But he asked me to find out from you, Saar."

"Go and tell him what you have seen. So far, the situation is alright."

He was quite content with my answer and moved away. I saw him crawling out through a gap in the barbed wire fencing and running towards the collector's office.

The brief interlude forced by the capable intelligence sleuth had distracted me from the proceedings outside. When I refocused on the affairs outside, I found that the speeches were almost over. The last speaker, the leader of the group, was now exhorting the crowd to enter the office forcibly.

Charged by the electrifying call of their leader, the crowd converged at the gate and the students started pushing against it with all their might. Our men on the inner side were pushing back. This tug-of-war continued for quite some time. Somehow, we managed to keep the gate closed and did not allow the students to push it open.

This necessitated a change of strategy by the demonstrators. Quite a few of them started climbing the gate and then jumped inside. There was perhaps one method by which we could have stopped them. When they had reached the top of the gate and were positioning themselves to take the jump, our men could have pushed them off to fall back on the other side.

Some quick thinking on my part made me realise that this could result in serious injuries. The idea was abandoned, and we decided to tackle them once they landed in our territory. The process of their climbing, jumping and landing, followed by our chasing and capturing them, was going on in full swing.

About fifteen to twenty of them had managed to accomplish their mission. Chasing and capturing them was becoming tedious. When this delicate operation was underway, I heard a strong whisper close to my ear, "Saar."

I was startled. I looked back and found someone in plain clothes very near me. This made me jump as I thought that one of the agitators had perhaps come near me. My jump took me slightly away from the man and gave me a chance to look at him properly. He was the same intelligence man.

"What?" I shouted at him.

"Saar, what is the situation?"

I had a cane in my hand. I was seriously contemplating whether I should give him a good blow with it when suddenly, Das *Babu*, a middle-aged sub-inspector, who was near me, caught hold of him.

Das *Babu* was someone who had seen the seamier side of policing and had, in the process, been badly treated, more so by our boss. He had never been given a good rating, had been punished on many occasions and was in a bad post. He was in a position where he had nothing to lose. After catching hold of the man's arm in a strong grip, he proceeded to firmly put his hands on his shoulders and shook him roughly.

"Hey! Why are you repeatedly coming here?"

"Saar, the SP has sent me to find out about the situation."

"Don't they have toilets in the collectorate?"

The intelligence man, by now, was in a state of shock.

"Go and tell the SP to use the toilet if he is so terrified. We are doing fine here."

There was a meek nod from the captive.

"If I see you here again, I will break your leg," were Das *Babu*'s final words to him.

The sleuth bolted from the scene. Having got rid of this nosey intruder, we once again focussed on the agitators. Most of them had been apprehended. Those outside had, by now, started losing steam and were rapidly dispersing. It was time for us to open the gate and chase the remaining agitators away. After completing the mop-up operations, we left the place.

I had a nagging suspicion that something was not right. There was no call from the SP, appreciating what we had done. What if the intelligence man had reported verbatim to the SP about his disastrous second visit? The SP would have never taken kindly, the advice of using a toilet. These thoughts nagged me. My fears came true when, in the evening, I got a letter, asking me to explain as to how the agitators could manage to get inside.

Receiving such letters had become quite a regular affair for me and required a measured response. I thought that an immediate reply might not be a very balanced one. At such moments, it was always better to consult someone else. After all, two minds were better than one.

On these occasions, I would seek help from the Additional SP, Mr Raj. We would sit together, almost every evening, drafting suitable replies to these memos, which I was receiving with alarming regularity. Raj, I had a feeling, had started to enjoy these drafting sessions. Then came his turn. It was not a memo, but a graver tragedy that shook him to the core.

A place close to Cuttack City, fortunately outside my jurisdiction, had an almost archaic industrial unit. It was not doing well. Issues like timely payment to the workers became not only a problem for the management but also the administration. The workers, led by their trade union, planned a massive protest at the site.

A serious problem was anticipated. Our boss, very consistent with his managerial concept, chose to again follow the 'push from behind' method. Since the area was out of my jurisdiction, he had to settle for Mr Raj. So, Raj went to the place with a group of policemen and was supposed to prevent any violence.

Those were the days when instant communication was not easy. However, we could gather that the situation was not under control. There was violence as anticipated and the crowd of agitators had run amuck. One policeman was badly mauled and injured as were quite a few others. Mr Raj came back with his uniform torn, his face swollen and his mood touching rock bottom. He refused to divulge anything and remained in a state of complete silence.

Later, the gory details started unfolding. It seemed that the unruly agitators were hell-bent on creating trouble. They pelted stones at the police party and started advancing. A few policemen went forward to assess the situation when one of them was dragged away by the crowd.

He was badly assaulted. At this point, the policemen requested Raj to order them to take action by resorting to a baton charge. For some strange reason, Raj preferred to remain silent. The policemen were getting restive, seeing one from among them being badly beaten. They kept on repeating their request for an order to take action, but Raj was equally persistent in his resolve to remain silent.

Whether he was scared to give orders or totally dumbfounded by the course of events was difficult to say, but the policemen had by now lost their patience. They surrounded Raj and shook him up. Still being unable to break his silence, they decided to move to the next level of delivering blows and kicks. Some even pulled at his uniform, resulting in the shirt pockets and the shoulder lapels getting dislodged from their normal places and hanging like the tongues of a pack of thirsty dogs.

At this stage, help arrived at the spot and some seasoned Deputy SP led the men, rescued the badly mauled policeman and restored some sanity. Raj returned, thoroughly shaken. I never had the heart to ask him about the incident or find out whether he had received a memo. I was quite content with my memos.

***

I had to spend a lot of time in the company of inspectors and other officers. It was very easy to deal with them and in the process, learn a lot about policing. Some of these officers were exceptionally good in their work and had built up a strong reputation. One such officer was Bhagawan *Babu*, who headed the most important police station.

One day, both of us were overseeing the arrangements made for a function of the Telugu community called Bonalu. It was almost midnight, and the festivities were in full swing. Bhagawan *Babu* and I decided to move out of the crowded area and chose a quiet place behind the festival *pandal*. It had been an extremely tiring evening for both of us. We were quietly relaxing, when I saw someone painted like a tiger, with a long tail, walking towards us. Just to get rid of the boredom, I said, "Bhagawan *Babu*, there is a tiger."

Bhagawan *Babu*, who had possibly dosed off, sprang up, looked at that person and shouted, "Hey, tiger?"

Seeing a uniformed policeman, the tiger stopped in his tracks and folded his hands.

"Where are you going?"

"Sir, I am going to answer nature's call," the tiger replied.

"Go."

The tiger was dismissed. This event cheered up an otherwise boring evening. Bhagawan *Babu*, after his short interlude with the tiger, was now alert and communicative. I thought it was a good moment to gather some information from him.

"Bhagawan *Babu*?"

"Yes, Sir."

"You have such an excellent reputation. Have you ever received any punishment?"

"I have, Sir."

"You have?"

"Yes, Sir."

"But why?"

"Sir, policing is quite a difficult business."

"But you are so proficient in policing. How could someone punish you?"

"Sir, it happened when I was a sub-inspector. I was posted as in charge of a rural police station."

"Where?" I wanted to know.

"It was Champua in Keonjhar District."

"Then?"

"SP Keonjhar, Sri Ghosh, came for inspection."

"Did he find any fault in your work?"

"Sir, it was not related to the police station. The inspection never happened."

"Why?"

"It was all my fault, Sir."

"What happened?"

"I was told that the SP is fond of angling. So, I had made arrangements for him near a big pond."

"Then?"

"I had built a small bamboo platform so that he could get close to the water and fish properly."

"Excellent."

"No, Sir. That was the cause of my trouble."

"Oh! How?"

"Sir, when the SP threw his line and settled on the chair, the platform suddenly collapsed."

"Collapsed?"

"Yes, Sir. It collapsed, and the SP fell inside the pond. We had to pull him out. He left Champua immediately after."

"Bhagawan *Babu,* it must have been really bad for you."

"Sir, it was a terrible mistake on my part. I was censured. That is the only punishment I have got to date."

"Really sad, Bhagawan *Babu.*"

"It happens, Sir."

We parted company on this rather sad note.

***

There were many instances where I had carried out my own operations without any direction from the SP. These were really professionally satisfying. Catching bootleggers and black marketeers or raiding gambling dens were part of these operations.

Once, we embarked on an operation to detect the illegal sale of liquor. It had become quite a nuisance as small shops had opened near localities of low-income labour-class people. They used to spend all their hard-earned money in the evening on this liquor, resulting in serious issues in their families.

Raj, the Additional SP, also volunteered to come along. We planned to go to a particular shop about which we had information. We parked our vehicles at a distance so that we could take them by surprise. The moment we got out of our vehicle and started walking towards our target, Raj started waving his baton all around him like a fan.

I was at the receiving end of a blow as I was close to him, which made me move away and keep a safe distance from him. Usually, a baton is used when you chase some miscreant or have to discipline some recalcitrant element, but here was an unusual situation where the man was using his baton without any consideration, treating friends and foes alike.

He kept on moving the baton at a good speed. It seemed that he had devised this method for his self-defence after his very tragic experience at the hands of his own men a few months earlier. This unpleasant experience must have made him realise that friends could be more dangerous than foes.

Well, whatever the reason, it was a wise move to get as far away from him as possible. So, I quickened my pace and walked towards the shop. I reached it much before the others. We were all in plain clothes. I saw a line of customers inside the shop, waiting for their turn to fill their glasses.

One could easily make out that most of them were in line for repeat orders as they looked quite inebriated. A couple of them looked quite intimidating with their bloodshot eyes. There was a small window through which glasses were filled and payments made. There was also a door by the side, which was locked from inside. I knocked on the door.

"Hey!" There was a loud call, followed by someone gripping my hand.

I looked back and found that it was one of the customers with bloodshot eyes. He looked at me for quite some time with absolute scorn and contempt. I was reminded of an incident in college when a sozzled classmate of mine had caught hold of my neck and almost choked me before others could rescue me.

He shouted, "Can't you see there is a line?"

I kept looking at him.

"Come and stand behind and wait for your turn."

I ignored him and knocked harder. By then, Raj and the others had entered the shop from the back and had caught hold of the seller. They opened the door from inside. The man with the bloodshot eyes released my hand from his grip. His expression had changed from scorn and contempt to one of disbelief.

"Wah!" he said and kept on looking at me. "Wah!" he repeated.

I looked away from him before he could come up with another 'Wah!'

However, he was not one to get away from so easily. "Wah!" he said again. "What a wonderful plan! You come from the front and knock on the door and others come from behind. Wah!"

I was quite impressed that he, intoxicated as he was, could discern the finer points of police tactics.

He continued with his 'wahs'. We went ahead with our work of arresting the vendor and seizing the stock. Raj was in a happy mood, having led a successful raid. Having spent quite some time with this group of policemen, he had probably realised that they were not the attacking types. Hence, he had suspended his cane movement, much to our collective relief.

***

We were faced with a similar situation a few days later when we went on a raid to arrest black marketeers of cinema tickets. Those were the days when watching a movie was possibly the only source of entertainment. There was no television or smartphones. Whenever a new film was playing in any hall, there used to be large crowds.

A group of persons, certainly with the connivance and help of the theatre owners, used to appropriate a large chunk of the tickets and sell them at exorbitant rates. On receiving information that rampant black marketing was going on in one particular hall, I decided to go there with a team. We reached the place and soon mingled in the crowd as normal ticket seekers.

Strangely, we could not find any black marketeer. I was quite surprised by this turn of events. Certainly, someone from the local police station must have leaked information about our raid. It was quite disturbing. I decided to leave, and the others followed. We got into our vehicles parked at a distance and drove off.

Once we got to a safe distance, I stopped my vehicle and got down. The other vehicle also stopped. We decided to walk back to the same hall again. When we reached there, I found a man on the steps of the hall, shouting, “Come back! Come back! Those police rascals have left.”

He kept abusing the police and progressed to much harsher expletives. I approached him from behind and caught hold of him. The black marketeers, confident that we had left, had let their guard down and were doing business with gay abandon. The others in our team could easily spot them. We were able to catch them with bunches of tickets and money.

They were put in our vehicles and we proceeded to the police station. The leader was in my vehicle. When I looked back at him, he was sitting with folded hands, looking very dejected. As we started moving, he said, “Hit me! Hit me hard!” He was pleading with one of our men. “Such senior officers had come, and I abused them? Hit me hard.”

No one took any notice of his rambling. After some time, he asked, “Sir, can I go now?”

By then, we had reached the police station. He quietly got down and went inside.

***

People like him and the man with the bloodshot eyes were the source of great entertainment in the otherwise drab surroundings. They made me forget the memos and spurred me on to embark on more such adventures.

Going on night rounds and checking various guards at night was part of my responsibility. One night, I went out for a round and after visiting various places, reached the office of the state vigilance. There was a guard of one head constable and six constables deployed in the office for guard duties.

It was around 2 a.m. and in the still surroundings of the night, my jeep, an old machine, entered the premises, making quite a noise. I thought this should be enough to rouse the guards. I asked my driver to stop the jeep at a distance of about twenty-five metres from the main building. I got down from the jeep and saw the sentry waking up from sleep and running and hiding behind a pillar. The usual practice is that when the sentry sees someone at night, he is to challenge him, shouting, "Halt! Who comes there?"

I was waiting for the sentry to challenge me, but there was not a sound from him. It was quite a unique situation, and I did not know how to break this impasse. My driver had by now got down and even he was quite concerned about the developments. It was then that I decided to shout at the sentry.

"Sentry! Sentry!"

He peeped out from behind the pillar.

"Where is the guard?" I asked.

"Guard! Guard!" he shouted.

I saw some movement as a few men came out and took positions behind other pillars. They were preparing for a big battle, it seemed.

Instead of lining up, they stood behind the pillars, pointing their rifles at both of us and following us with the muzzles as we shifted position. This was turning out to be a terrible situation.

I was reminded of the incident when a DSP got shot by a guard in a border outpost during checking of the guard at night. In his case, there was no verbal challenge but just a shot fired at him. Here was a situation where these idiots could fire multiple shots at me. My driver, an old hand, was also getting restive as even he had not experienced such a situation earlier. We looked at each other and he decided to end the matter.

"Rascals!" he shouted. "The ASP is here for a round. Stand in a line."

His admonition had a startling effect. Four of them emerged from behind the pillars and stood in a line. I went forward and found that of the seven deployed in the office, only four were present and the others had gone home. This was the state of preparedness of the guards in a city that had the police headquarters. I gave my report to the SP the next day. I never got to know what he did about it.

I soon got my promotion orders and had to leave, having learnt a lot about how to work with a malignant boss.

# Public Speaking

"What?" Mr Lenka blurted, looking absolutely shocked. "You want to take charge today?"

"Yes, Sir."

I had travelled overnight in a bus from Bhubaneswar to reach Koraput in the morning. Having called on the SP, I proceeded to meet Mr Lenka, the Additional SP, to take charge from him.

"Yes, Sir?" he retorted. "Don't you know that the Chief Justice is touring the district?"

"What has that got to do with my taking charge?"

"What has that got to do with it?" He looked at me as if I was a complete idiot. "There will be a vacuum in the district."

"Vacuum?"

"Yes. You are totally inexperienced. How will you handle his visit? Anyway, come and have dinner with me."

I was baffled. I had thought that Koraput, being far away from a happening city like Cuttack, would be a place where I could properly settle down, but here was a man talking about a vacuum. I went to the SP to seek his advice. He smiled and told me to take things easy and take charge after a couple of days.

I came back to my room in the guest house. Fortunately, Khanna, the ASP, was also lodged in the same guest house. He had, by then, spent about seven to eight months in Koraput and was aware of many things. I narrated to him my unsuccessful attempt to join and also about the invitation to dinner.

"Dinner with Mr Lenka?"

"Yes, he has invited me. Why don't you also come?"

Khanna did not look very pleased but agreed to accompany me. We reached Mr Lenka's place in the evening. His house was a total mess and looked unkempt. He was staying here alone, leaving his wife and children in the village. We were asked to sit, and he joined us soon, dressed in a *lungi* and a *banian*.

He settled down on a chair, lifted his *lungi* above his knees and stretched his legs on the small table in front of him. His unsightly legs were on full display before us. Since it was a social evening, there was no mention of the contentious issue of handing and taking over charge. Once his legs were properly aired, he started his long monologue.

It covered quite a few instances of his heroic deeds as a police officer, which included his exceptional handling of law and order, VIP visits and his abilities in crime control. Then he looked at his legs (he seemed to be in love with them) and said, "See how strong they are. I have seen many hard postings."

We were listening to him.

"One of the most difficult was my posting in Dum Duma."

"Dum Duma?" I asked.

"Yes. I was in charge of the company of armed police of the 1st Battalion."

"Oh!" It was Khanna's turn to add to the one-sided conversation.

"We were trained in guerrilla warfare."

"Why?" We both wanted to know.

"We were supposed to fight the Chinese."

"Chinese?"

"Yes. Dum Duma is very close to the China border. That training has really made me strong."

Before we could react and elicit some information about his encounters, if any, with the Chinese, he caught hold of poor Khanna's hand and placed it on his calf.

"See how hard and strong it is."

I don't remember if Khanna actually pressed his calf muscle to ascertain its hardness, but I saw him pull away his hand in utter disgust. The evening was certainly not progressing well.

Finally, dinner was served. There was an item that looked like mutton curry. I saw Khanna taking a piece and then making a face as if he had put something rotten in his mouth. He took it out immediately. My keen observation of Khanna's reaction saved me from a similar fate. I didn't touch the item at all. Mr Lenka was too engrossed in eating to even look at us. He seemed to be enjoying the mutton.

Finally, our torture ended. While walking back to the guest house, I asked Khanna, "How was that mutton?"

"Cchah! It was horrible! So smelly! I think it was rat meat."

"Rat?"

"Yes, I think so. Cchah!"

"He must have been trained to eat rats during his guerrilla training," I said.

We had a hearty laugh and walked back to our rooms.

The Chief Justice had not yet completed his tour; hence, my waiting period continued. That evening, when Khanna and I were taking a stroll, someone came running towards us.

"Sir!" he said excitedly. "The DSP's wife has fallen into the well."

"What!" We both exclaimed and started running towards the DSP's house.

By the time we reached, she had been safely retrieved but was not in a position to talk to anyone. The DSP, Mr Mohanty, however, was quite unfazed and was narrating the sequence of events as to how his dear wife had been led by some ethereal apparition to the well. From the way he was narrating the episode, it seemed that he had vast experience of these visits from the land of spirits and knew about their moods and behaviour to the finest detail.

Both of us found the whole situation a bit spooky. Later, however, rumours started making the rounds that the poor lady, fed up with her husband's philandering, had plunged into the well to put an end to her misery. Anyway, no one thought much of prying into the affairs of the family.

Having heard in detail from the DSP about spirits and ghosts freely roaming in the town, we came back to our rooms. As I was about to retire for the night, suddenly, the lights started flickering and one of the bulbs exploded with a loud bang, sending shivers down my spine. I had a terrible night.

"What's happening, Khanna?" I was full of concern the next morning. Not being able to take charge, the horrible dinner, ghosts leading people to the well and finally, the exploding bulb, was all too much for me.

"You must take charge today," Khanna advised me.

I went with a strong resolve and met Mr Lenka. He had some other issues, which he wanted to take care of before handing over the charge to me. This time, the SP was firm, and I finally took charge.

Things got much better once I became engrossed in my work. Soon, I realised that the place was indeed a paradise. It was a quaint little town on the hills of the Eastern Ghats at an elevation of approximately 3000 feet. It had lovely weather all year round and incessant rains during monsoons.

The friendly people, excellent colleagues and above all, the SP, a gem of a person, who took great care in mentoring me, added to my bliss. He had a wonderful sense of humour and one could really enjoy his company for hours. The district magistrate was an excellent person, too. The entire group was like family to me.

The population of the district was mainly tribal. The tribes are a group of self-respecting people, free from the ills of modern society, straightforward, honest and far away from greed and avarice. It was, hence, quite easy to deal with crime and law and order issues.

Koraput town has a great tradition of sports, football and volleyball being the most popular games. There were quite a few excellent players in the police, who were almost adored by the town people. I had a great time joining them in their games. The volleyball court was situated very close to the bus stand and hence, used to draw lots of onlookers when even friendly games were played.

This was a perfect environment for work and peaceful contemplation. Being a small town, one could closely observe officers from other departments and how they went about discharging their responsibilities. It was also an opportunity to be associated with senior police officers, especially the DIG, when they toured the town. There were quite a few incidents involving various categories of officers, which helped me a lot in my pursuit of excellence.

The district judge for Koraput, for some strange reason, had his headquarters in Jeypore, a town about twenty kilometres down the hill. After my joining, I called on him and found him to be a man of exceptional qualities – soft-spoken, willing to listen and above all, amenable to suggestions for improving coordination.

I remember that in those days, the district judge was not even provided with a vehicle. He would invariably take a bus from Jeypore to Koraput to attend meetings. He was respected by all and I looked up to him. He was a person who demonstrated that respect had to be earned and did not come to you because of your position.

I had a chance of encountering another gentleman of the same rank who was a total contrast. He held a state-level post and had come on tour in his official vehicle. Having completed his official task, he decided to go to Jeypore to attend a social function. His driver and he were proceeding for the event in great haste when the driver, for some reason, drove the vehicle on the wrong side of a traffic post.

The traffic constable on duty, a simple tribal, true to his oath to safeguard the law, whistled vigorously for the driver to stop. The driver, having driven in Bhubaneswar and with a judge in the back seat, ignored the whistling and continued with his act of misdemeanour.

This traffic constable, however, was made of sterner stuff than the ones in Bhubaneswar. On seeing that his whistling had no effect, he probably remembered his oath once again and in a swift move, he jumped from his pedestal in the middle of the road and stood in front of the offending vehicle.

The driver and more so, the judge, was temporarily stunned by this unforeseen development. Recovering from the shock and still finding the constable blocking their way, the judge decided that it was time to set him straight.

The judge was dressed for the social function in a traditional *dhoti* and *kurta*. Thus attired, he alighted from the car and marched towards the constable. What followed was unclear, but it appeared that there was a heated discussion. The judge started explaining, with some amount of authority, the position of law, but the constable remained quite firm in his resolve to prevent further infringement on his watch.

The judge started to lose his temper, more so because quite a few passers-by had gathered around and were interestedly watching the episode of top-class law enforcement. At this stage, the judge, probably in his excitement and anger, switched over to English and started admonishing the constable.

The constable, not very proficient in the language of the Britishers, could not make out much of what was happening. He realised that the matter was beyond him and the intervention of higher ranks was an immediate necessity. He directed the judge to proceed to the police station. Strangely, this instruction did not shock the judge, as he had, by then, possibly crossed the threshold of being shocked that morning.

He started following the constable towards the police station located about a hundred metres from the scene. The onlookers, who did not want to miss the finale of this interesting episode, decided to join the march, too. The constable, followed by the judge and then the onlookers, marched towards the police station.

While the constable marched in silence with his strong resolve to uphold the law, the judge, not content with his short admonition, continued to shout at the constable in fluent and flowing English, questioning his mental abilities, poor training and total ignorance of the principles of law.

After a while, they had reached the police station when the judge sighted an officer standing on the station veranda. On seeing him, he stopped and in a loud voice, commanded, "Sub-Inspector, write down what I say!"

Now, a sub-inspector is a big man inside his police station. He is used to being treated with respect. This sudden and loud command from a *dhoti*-clad man on the street was unexpected. He was not shocked but felt deeply insulted. In his profession, he had been exposed to many types of people, but this was unprecedented. With a look of disgust, he asked the constable, "Who is this fellow?"

The constable, fuming from the barrage of English insults, was happy to have received the attention of the higher rank so quickly and replied immediately, "Sir, do you see how he is behaving with you? Just imagine what he would have done to me."

This lead was enough for the sub-inspector. Without much ado, he caught hold of the judge, pulled him towards the lock-up, opened the iron grill door, pushed him inside and bolted the door.

There was total silence as the judge was perhaps dumbfounded. This was a contingency he had never anticipated. However, before anything further could happen, the inspector, who had his office nearby, came to the station. His eyes fell on the judge in the lock-up and he shrieked in disbelief. He had, during some earlier posting, known the judge and recognised him at once.

The lock-up was opened, and the judge was solemnly escorted out, made to sit and offered water, tea and profuse apologies. He remained silent as he was perhaps still in a state of shock. Only after the local DSP arrived at the spot and he was alone with him did the judge open up.

The DSP, Mr Padhi, started with apologies and reminded the judge of how he had taught them the Evidence Act during their training.

"So, Padhi *Babu,* this is the *gurudakshina* that you had to give me."

"No, Sir. It was a genuine mistake. They were confused by your attire."

"My attire, eh?"

Padhi kept silent.

By this time, the judge's temper had cooled. After a short spell of silence, he confided, "Padhi *Babu,* as soon as the sub-inspector locked the door, I thought I was finished."

Fortunately, the nearly finished judge decided to end the matter there and proceeded to attend his social function.

For me, this turned out to be a classic case study of what a haughty ego can do to you.

During my posting in Koraput, there were several occasions when the SP was not available, which made me interact closely with the DIG. As the DIG was located at Berhampur, a good two hundred and fifty kilometres away, one had to interact with him on the phone and through correspondence.

Once every couple of months, the DIG visited Koraput for some inspection or supervision. During my tenure, I had the chance to work under two DIGs. Strangely, they were a study in contrast, too.

The DIG, who was in position when I joined, was known as an officer of sterling reputation. He was impeccably honest, extremely proficient in his work and a person you could look up to. He was one who would tell you to your face what he felt and admonish you if necessary. He had a really short temper and would blow up suddenly.

At times, an outburst of anger would be followed by an overpowering urge to deliver a good slap or a blow. Though no one could readily recollect any incident where he had actually slapped any officer, there were many instances where he had reached the stage of raising his hand in a rage.

My predecessor, Mr Lenka, I was told, had been a victim of his rage many a time and had to take swift remedial action to escape physical contact. However, other ranks, especially his drivers, were not so lucky.

At times, while seated in his car, if he was jolted by sudden braking or a swerve of the vehicle, he would invariably deliver a strong slap to the occipital region of the driver, throwing him into a state of confusion and despair. There were instances when the bewildered driver got down from the car and fled the scene, leaving the DIG stranded.

Anyway, this gentleman once decided to come to Koraput when the SP was away and wanted to inspect the DSP's office in a place called Malkangiri. The DSP in Malkangiri, Das, was an officer who, over the years, had worked with single-minded devotion in building up a reputation of being a lazy and unprofessional oaf, equally disliked by both superiors and subordinates.

The DIG was also aware of his sterling qualities and possibly wanted to confirm the same through a personal visit. Such being the delicate task at hand, I was to accompany the DIG in the absence of the SP.

Malkangiri was a fairly long drive. The DIG was very communicative and discussed many matters on the way. It was a pleasure interacting with him and learning a lot from his experience. The driver drove to the satisfaction of the DIG and there was no occasion for tempers to rise.

We reached Malkangiri and the next morning, the inspection was to commence. We reached the office and found Das standing in front of it, attired in a ceremonial tunic, with his staff lined up behind him. As the DIG approached, he came forward to report to him. In addition to all his other qualities, he had a habit of stammering.

On facing the DIG, I could see that he was struggling to say something, but no words came out of his mouth. The DIG, never before having encountered such a situation, looked at me. I politely explained that Das stammered.

"Oh!"

Das somehow managed to mumble something and the ritual of reporting ended. We went inside and the inspection began. The quality of his supervision of cases and inspection notes was examined. The DIG was not very happy with the quality. He pointed out the shortcomings and asked the DSP to take note.

He now decided to test the DSP's knowledge by asking him a couple of questions. The first one was about a register and why it was maintained. The DSP thought for some time and responded with a silly reply. I could sense that something would go wrong because on hearing the reply, the DIG's rate of breathing increased.

The second question followed, related to the same register. This time, the DSP's reply was even more absurd.

The DIG exploded, "Idiot!"

The DSP, who must have been well aware of the DIG's temper and his propensity to slap, was rather well prepared for this contingency. Even before the DIG could finish saying the word, Das dashed off. We could see him running out of the door and after a while, turn sharply to the right and vanish from our view.

The DIG, it seemed, was not a great believer in the doctrine of hot pursuit. He made no attempt to follow him despite the urge to slap still tormenting him. He looked at me and started shouting as to how we had pampered this joker. I remained quiet and the DIG also gradually cooled down. He ordered the orderly constable, "Go! Get that idiot!"

The orderly did not have to go far because the idiot was possibly lurking near the window. He came in with a sheepish grin.

"Sit down," the DIG commanded.

Das sat down, breathing heavily and on the edge of the chair, fully prepared for another sprint if required. The inspection ended soon after and we returned. I had my own first-hand experience of the DIG's temper.

The next DIG who took charge a couple of months later was a different cup of tea. He was suave, spoke well and little and kept to himself. He was not highly spoken of for his professional knowledge or conduct. Many had red-flagged him as one who could let anyone down if his own personal interest was involved. I had been warned to be extremely careful while dealing with him. I did not have to wait too long to observe his true qualities.

We received information that a small group of Naxalites were moving into the Malkangiri area and going from village to village. The problem had raised its ugly head in the neighbouring state, but no activities or incidents had been reported on our side. It was, hence, a matter of concern for us when we got this information.

I proceeded to the area and visited the villages. When I reached one of them, I got information that a group had indeed come there and left for another village a day earlier. We rushed to the next village, only to find that they had left a day or in some cases, a few hours earlier. This cat-and-mouse game continued for around a week.

Thereafter, information about their movement dried up. We assumed that they would have crossed the border and gone back. I returned to Koraput and promptly informed the DIG of the details of my visit. I had really toiled a lot in those seven days and expected some words of encouragement, but he only listened and kept mum.

Since it was a very important matter, I thought it would be appropriate to inform the DGP as well. I informed him of the incident and my visit. Being a sharp officer, he understood the situation fairly well and asked me to activate a good information network in the area.

I thought the matter had ended, but the next day, I got a call from the DIG. He sounded very disturbed.

"I am starting for Koraput and will be there by lunchtime."

"Why so suddenly, Sir?"

"Just be there and meet me," he almost shouted at me.

"Sure, Sir."

I had no clue about his sudden visit. He was not the kind of person who would travel such a long distance unless there was something.

The mystery was soon solved when I got a call from Cuttack to find out whether the DIG had reached. It so happened that soon after I spoke to the DG about the visit of the Naxalites, the DIG had also called him and given him a detailed account of the issue.

Being an officer who firmly believed that it was the solemn duty of a superior to only find fault with his subordinates, he had told the DG that the Additional SP had made it a point to reach a village only after the Naxalites had left. It was his firm conclusion that with proper planning, the Additional SP could have easily apprehended them.

The DG was a man of sharp intellect. He had gathered all the information from me when I had spoken to him. He directed the DIG to immediately proceed there and do all he could with his advanced methods of planning.

The DIG had never expected that he would land in such a predicament. It was a classic case of a man falling into his own trap. The DG had also directed him that he was not to take me with him as there were other issues at Koraput that required my immediate attention.

The trapped DIG reached Koraput and looked totally shaken at the turn of events. I knew he was to proceed further but did not bring up the subject.

Soon he said, "I have to go to Malkangiri to study the Naxalite issue."

"To Malkangiri, Sir?"

"Yes. I will leave soon after lunch."

"Right, Sir."

"You have to arrange for my escort."

"Escort?"

He looked quite irritated with my question and snapped, "Yes. Don't you require escorts?"

I had taken four men in my jeep when I had gone.

"Oh! Organise one platoon (thirty men) to accompany me."

"Platoon?" I was shocked.

"Don't give me that look. A platoon will follow me."

"Sure, Sir. I will organise it."

"Yes, and I will need a personal weapon."

"Will a revolver suffice?"

He thought for some time, probably trying to recollect what a revolver looked like and then said, "Yes. Everything should be ready soon. I will leave in an hour."

Within the stipulated time, the platoon, seated in a troop carrier and the armourer, with the revolver, had reached the circuit house. The DIG came out and on seeing him, the sub-inspector jumped out of the troop carrier, marched towards him and reported, "Sir, platoon ready to accompany you, Sir."

Seeing the sub-inspector in his uniform with a revolver in his holster and a pouch carrying ammunition on his belt, the DIG was visibly shaken. He probably realised that he was now on the verge of going into a battle without the slightest clue of what he was about to face. I could see him shaking slightly. He then looked at me and spoke in a quivering voice, "Where is my revolver?"

The armourer immediately appeared with a revolver and handed it to him.

"Is it loaded?"

"No, Sir."

"Why?"

"Sir, a weapon is never given loaded. This is the ammunition."

A packet of rounds was handed over to him. He tried different ways of opening the chamber of the revolver. His hands were shaking visibly. Being unsuccessful in his efforts, he looked pitiably at the armourer, who promptly took the revolver from him, loaded it and handed it back to him. This task was completed, and the DIG got into his vehicle.

He looked at me and said, "Give strict instructions to the platoon to be right behind my car."

"Yes, Sir."

He drove off with the troop carrier following him closely. I had a feeling that he would get into the troop carrier once he reached the forested area.

He returned after a couple of days. He did not utter a word about the Naxalites or his advanced methods of apprehending them and quietly went back to headquarters. He did not bother me much after this. He had learnt his lesson.

These two case studies of DIGs became valuable additions to my collection on behavioural analysis.

During my posting in Koraput, I was exposed to an incident that made me contemplate the various aspects of public speaking. I knew for certain that I did not have the gift of the gab, but also realised that sooner rather than later, one would have to stand behind a lectern and speak.

With so many functions being held in the district, there was heavy demand for officers to attend them and also address the gathering. The first such demand on me was made one evening when Professor Mukherjee, the principal of the local college, came to our house along with his wife. He was a respected man, and it was a great pleasure to host him at home. After an exchange of pleasantries, he revealed the purpose of his visit.

"Mr Mishra, I have come to you with a request."

"Sir, please tell me what I can do for you."

"I have come to invite you to be the chief guest at our college's annual function."

"Me?"

"Yes."

"But why me? There are so many senior functionaries available."

"Can I speak frankly?"

"Of course."

"You see, I want you as chief guest because you are a police officer."

"Oh!"

"Yes. The students will behave with restraint if you come."

Alarm bells started ringing in my head. I was reminded of an episode described in gory detail in a P. G. Wodehouse novel about Bertie Wooster attending a function in a girls' school. Just remembering what poor Bertie had to undergo in those moments made me extremely nervous.

The principal's invitation to face a pack of full-grown adults made me shiver, just imagining to what extent they would go. Having assessed the situation from all angles and being thankful for having read the aforementioned novel, I decided that it would be suicidal to accept the invitation. However, I did not want to disappoint the principal who had come to me with such hope.

"Sir, can you give me a couple of days? I will find an apt chief guest for you. If I do not find anyone, I will accept your invitation."

He looked disappointed at my reply but reluctantly agreed.

I determinedly embarked on my mission to look for a chief guest the next morning. After some thinking, I zeroed in on Mr Satpathy. He was from the teaching profession but was on deputation, heading a body meant to promote awareness among youth. What better way to spread awareness among them than to give a rousing address on their annual day?

I immediately proceeded to meet Mr Satpathy. Strategically, I did not mention the college matter immediately. We started discussing small matters and then I approached the core issue in a very subtle way.

"Satpathy *Babu,* I have heard that you were a very popular lecturer?"

"Not really. I used to prepare well for my classes," he replied with all modesty.

"You had an excellent reputation. You should not give up lecturing."

"You see, in my present job, there is more of administration and almost no teaching."

"The college is holding its annual function."

"Really?"

"Yes, and they are looking for an inspiring speaker as chief guest."

"Oh!"

"I think there cannot be anyone better than you for the purpose."

"Me?"

"Yes, you can really motivate the students with an inspiring talk."

"You think so?"

"You will be a smashing hit. The principal was keen to settle the matter of the choice of the chief guest early. I will request him to contact you."

"Okay. If you say so."

The matter was satisfactorily concluded. My second visit that morning was to the principal with this proposal.

"Mr Satpathy?" He did not sound very excited at the prospect.

"Yes."

"I would still prefer to have you, but if you insist, let it be Satpathy."

A great weight was lifted off me. The disaster had been successfully averted and soon, I forgot all about it.

About a week or ten days later, on a Sunday morning, I was in the thick of a very competitive volleyball match being played in the town. A large crowd had converged around the court, watching the proceedings with great interest. The game was reaching its final stage, and I was concentrating on watching the ball.

Suddenly, I saw a head bobbing up from within the crowd on my side and then going down. The movement was repeated quite a few times. I could not make out who it was as the exciting game did not allow me even a moment to look to the side. After some time, I found that the bobbing head had pushed through the crowd and come closer.

I looked towards it and found that it was Mr Satpathy. Once he realised that I had seen him, he started waving at me frantically and gesturing for me to come out of the court. The moment the game ended, he rushed into the court, grabbed my hand and pulled me to the side. This was rather unusual behaviour for a known pacifist. I saw that he had an absolutely shattered look on his face and the appearance of someone who had been deprived of sleep and peace of mind.

"What happened? Are you unwell?" I asked him concernedly.

"What happened?" His voice was loaded with heavy sarcasm. He looked at me with scorn and said, "You are a dangerous and untrustworthy person."

It was a terrible accusation, and I was unable to comprehend why he was so upset.

"What did I do?"

"What did you do? Didn't you ask me to go to the college's annual function as the chief guest?"

"Yes, I did," I admitted.

"You knew very well what was going to happen, didn't you?"

"What happened? I am sure your speech was good."

"You had asked me to give an inspiring speech."

"Yes, I did."

"I had prepared for almost three days for the speech."

"Very good."

"What is good about it? It was the cause of all my problems."

"Why?"

"I started my speech and was happy that it was going smoothly. After about five minutes, I reached a part of the speech where I had to quote Bertrand Russel."

"You quoted Bertrand Russel before this group?"

"Yes, it was a very relevant quote, but I think the problem started from there."

"Oh?"

"Yes, the moment I mentioned Bertrand Russel, someone from the audience shouted, '*Saala*.'"

"What? They called you *saala*?"

"Yes, it started with *saala*."

"Oh! Did you stop?"

"No, I carried on. There was some din and commotion going on, but I continued with my speech. I finished with Russel and wanted to move on to Churchill."

"You wanted to quote him, too?"

"Yes, it was a well-prepared speech, but the moment I mentioned Churchill, all the students started shouting, 'Churrrrr Chilllll.'"

"Oh!"

"This time, they did not just shout '*saala*'; they abused me badly, raising questions about my parents."

He was almost on the verge of breaking down.

"Then?" I asked.

"I tried to continue, but they rushed to the stage."

"You mean they came at you?"

"Yes. They called me a rascal and said I should leave."

"Oh?"

"They wanted their cultural programme to start immediately. I had to run from there and escape through the back door."

"What about the principal?"

"Principal? Why should I bother about him? It was both of you who pushed me into this. You knew this was going to happen, didn't you?"

He was pretty convinced that I had sent him on this dangerous mission, knowing fully well that it would end in disaster.

I had to do a lot of explaining to calm him. Frankly, I had never expected that things would come to a head in such a manner. We both agreed that the particular group of students did not deserve such an illuminating talk. He announced that he would never go to any annual function in the future.

This episode was an eye-opener for me and made me think hard about the issue of public speaking. My days at Koraput were drawing to a close, and I was soon transferred to another district as the SP. However, the memories of Koraput still linger on.

# Mr Fidgety

I was in Sector 3 police station in Rourkela when a call came from the DIG.

"I just came back from that rally, but I did not find either you or the Additional SP there."

His tone was quite accusatory. He was referring to a rally organised by a trade union to draw attention to some of their demands.

"Both the Additional SP and I had been to the rally and found hardly a hundred people participating in it. Since no problem was anticipated, the DSP was directed to handle it," I responded.

"What? DSP? You are new to Rourkela; here, all rallies have to be handled by the SP. I see that even the Additional SP is having a good time sitting in the police station."

I had joined Rourkela a few days ago. It was an industrial city with all the accompanying problems. The major issues were crime by interstate criminals and various law and order matters arising out of the steel plant. It was also communally very sensitive, having witnessed bloody riots in the sixties.

The DIG also had his office in Rourkela. I had come on transfer from Mayurbhanj, a district, which, fortunately, did not have a DIG posted in the same place. There, I could take a call on any matter, but here, things were turning out to be different and a bit dicey.

"Padhi *Babu*, what is all this?" I asked the Additional SP.

"Sir, the DIG has a habit of interfering with everything. One has to deal with him carefully," he advised.

I decided to nip this problem in the bud. I called the DIG and requested a meeting with him. I arrived at the appointed hour and politely told him that there were matters, which I should be allowed to deal with in my way. Of course, he could always step in when he wanted to, but he should stop bothering me on every matter.

He was a strange person. After listening to me, he quietly agreed to whatever I said. He appeared to me as a constipated person, not at all at ease with himself. Such kinds of persons are never to be taken at their face value. I, therefore, had a sneaking suspicion that he would soon forget about this conversation and be back to his old self, sooner rather than later.

I did not have long to wait.

My transfer and joining in Rourkela happened so suddenly that I did not have enough time to gather relevant and useful information about the DIG. The officers known to me were not very forthcoming on the subject either. This was perhaps because the DIG had spent a long time outside the state.

The only information that was doing the rounds was about a catastrophic event that had almost put him out of action for a considerable period. I had never heard of such an incident before. The sad incident being referred to was when a commode in the DIG's residence gave way and collapsed.

The breaking of a commode certainly cannot be categorised as dangerous. In this case, however, things took a rather serious turn and resulted in a profound tragedy as it broke when the DIG himself was perched on top and in the process of using it. Hearing his cries of agony, people rushed in and found him in a pool of blood with severe injuries. He had to be rushed to a hospital and extensive repair work, involving thirty-six stitches, to be precise, was required to restore him to shape.

When I heard of this incident, I was all sympathy for the DIG. Just imagine, a person in the process of relieving himself, suddenly finds the pot on which he sits, crumbling and sharp pieces of porcelain piercing his body. It must have been terrible.

I had concluded that it was definitely the fault of the public works department for placing such a sub-standard commode in the home of an important functionary with little concern for his safety. However, after meeting the DIG and having first-hand exposure to his constipated character, I quickly revised my opinion.

I was convinced that this fellow, in his state of constipation or maybe with a bout of irritable bowel syndrome, must have climbed onto the commode with his feet up on the seat rather than on the floor and to have a proper evacuation, exerted considerable pressure by way of jumping up and down on the commode, causing it to crash. After all, a commode is designed for a particular threshold of weight and certainly not for jumping loads.

The thought of working with such a superior pushed me into a state of melancholy, but I soon realised that there was no way out. The Additional SP and I decided to take things in our stride and deal with situations as and when they arose.

The inspection of a police station is supposed to be an important supervisory task. Even the DIG had to inspect his quota of police stations every year. It was an exercise that this gentleman used to love. It not only gave him the chance to lord over the particular police station for that day but also sit in the inspector's chair, the very chair from which all policing powers flowed.

It was also an opportunity for him to ensure my presence at the station, sit in front of him and witness the proceedings. As the inspection progressed, his expression clearly revealed that he was convinced I was a total nincompoop and needed to learn from his vast knowledge.

While a mute spectator to the goings-on, it suddenly struck me that this gentleman did not fall into any of the categories of inspecting officers that one had heard of. There were many officers, belonging to different ranks and departments, who were particularly fond of eating. For them, going on an inspection meant good food. The poor officer who had to organise the visit had not only to impress the inspecting officer's palate with the high quality of food but also the number of items served. I cannot readily recall if there was any record for the number of items served but have heard of instances when between thirty to forty different types of dishes were laid out for the inspecting officer to feast upon.

There was a particular officer of the rank of commissioner, who used to love this kind of arrangement. I had heard that once, during an inspection of the office of the Sub-Divisional Officer, he was given such a sumptuous lunch. Having eaten his fill, he retired for an afternoon siesta.

When the SDO went to pick him up from the rest house at around five in the evening to continue with the inspection, he found the window open. A shadow appeared from behind the thin curtain for a few seconds and then disappeared. This was repeated a few times.

Curious about what was happening inside the room, the SDO went to the door and found it unlocked. In his anxiety to see if things were alright, he pushed the door open and went inside. He found the great officer, dressed in a *dhoti* tied up to his waist, making it appear like short underpants, holding the railings of the window and busy doing rhythmic squats.

"The lunch was very nice. You see, a bit of exercise helps in good digestion," he explained.

"Sir, shall we go to the office now?"

"Yes, yes. I will be ready in a minute. By the way, will the same cook be preparing dinner also?"

"Yes, Sir."

"Good."

So, it was all about the food. This very gentleman was once on a visit to a small place named Titlagarh and was invited for lunch by three sub-collectors under training there. These officers had some prior information about his love for food, but being young and idealistic, they decided on a menu, which they thought was certainly princely.

The menu, which was approved after much deliberation, comprised rice, dal and a vegetable curry. The star item of the repast was to be egg curry. It was decided that since the commissioner loved non-vegetarian food, there should be two eggs, instead of the usual one, per person. The three of them and the guest made up a party of four, so eight eggs would be sufficient.

The commissioner was received with due courtesy and taken straight to the dining room. He started enquiring about their training and related matters. At this stage, the cook started placing the food items on the table. Unfortunately, the bowl containing the precious egg curry was placed close to the commissioner.

Alerted by the smell emanating from the dish, he lifted its lid and found the eggs. Placing the lid aside on the table, he picked up one egg and popped it into his mouth. The talk on training continued. He picked up another egg. This one perhaps had a vigorously stimulating effect on his system, for he just could not stop himself after that.

The third, fourth and fifth eggs flew into his mouth in quick succession. The three sub-collectors were looking at each other with utter disbelief. As the conversation progressed, the remaining three eggs also met the same fate. Having finished, he placed the lid back, pushed the bowl away, stretched his arms and back and ordered, "Let the food be served."

The poor sub-collectors, who had kept a count of their precious eggs, were too stunned to understand what they had witnessed. What food will they serve? After exchanging bewildered glances, one of them blurted out the truth, "Sir, we had got only egg curry prepared for lunch."

The commissioner took some time to register this catastrophic reply. All that the sub-collectors heard him say was "Oh", followed by silence, then another louder "Oh", followed by more silence and finally, a third even louder "Oh". Each "Oh" signified his level of frustration and disappointment as the information slowly started sinking in. He was now staring at the prospect of leaving without lunch.

However, he was a benign man. Even deprived of his food, he maintained his calm. The subject of discussion now shifted from training to how young officers should learn to organise good food and what constitutes a good menu.

"Eggs are good as starters," was his final advice.

There were others who were not nearly as benign. They would enjoy the lavish food but were merciless in finding faults during inspection. In fact, they took a lot of pride in it and bragged about the number of mistakes they could detect. It gave them great pleasure in recalling how the poor officer had to plead for mercy.

An incident involving one such officer was once narrated to me by a seasoned DSP. The inspecting officer happened to be the circle inspector who had gone to inspect a police station. The sub-inspector who was in charge of the police station had made arrangements for the inspector to stay in the inspection room on the police station premises.

The sub-inspector was well aware of the notorious habits of the inspector. Usually, the inspection is carried out for two days. This particular inspector had a habit of enjoying his food on the first day while keeping the ruthless act of finding faults for the second day. The clever sub-inspector had kept this important time schedule well in his mind and prepared accordingly.

Soon after the inspection started, hot *pakoras* were served along with the first cup of tea. The inspector believed in quality as well as quantity. So, the *pakoras* had to be hot and crispy. Several rounds of *pakoras,* with pieces of green chillies, were served straight from the pan. As the rounds progressed, the quantity of green chillies kept on increasing.

The tangy taste of chillies in the crispy hot *pakoras* was going down well with him. Once hooked to them, the inspector could not stop himself. Finally, having consumed a load of these chilli-laced *pakoras,* it was time for a break from eating. The inspection continued till lunchtime.

Equal care was taken to prepare the lunch. The mutton curry was perfectly cooked with the best of spices and a dash of red chillies. As the lunch progressed, more mutton was served. Each successive helping was loaded with more and more red chilli powder.

Having eaten his fill, the inspector retired for his afternoon siesta.

The next stage of inspection started around five in the evening. A spicy mixture was served along with tea. A similar strategy of red chillies in the mixture had been planned. The amount of chilli powder in the mixture kept on steadily increasing. Towards the end of the session, the mixture that was served was mostly chilli powder. The evening inspection ended, and it was time to rest and prepare for dinner.

The deadly combination of green chillies in the morning and copious amounts of red chilli powder in the afternoon had started to act on the system of the inspector. Even though he was not feeling too well, he just could not forego the dinner. The temptation of fish and chicken in delicious gravy simply could not be ignored.

Soon after dinner, he retired for the night.

All hell broke loose around midnight. The inspection room was suddenly ablaze with light and the police station staff woke up to the sound of "Ho, ho, ho, ho!" They saw the inspector running to the toilet. He returned after some time. The lights were switched off, but not for long. Very soon, the "Ho, ho, ho, ho" was heard again, and the inspector was seen running back to the toilet. He returned, but this time, there was no scope to even switch off the lights before he ran back to the toilet.

These quick sprints to the toilet and back continued for a long time. At daybreak, the poor inspector was seen lying in a pitiable condition, bleary-eyed, clutching his stomach now and then and totally dehydrated. It was decided that he would leave for his headquarters immediately.

The second day of the inspection was successfully averted and the sub-inspector was saved from the misery in store for him. His research on the combination of green and red chillies and its effect on the digestive system had worked to absolute perfection.

There was another type of inspection officers who were not foodies but completed their work without any fuss. Here also, there were the punishing types and the benign ones. Not much material is available on their exploits.

The DIG fell into the benign category in this group. He was too senior to carry out an inspection for even a day. Half a day was good enough for him, but even that duration was proving to be hell for me. Things were getting extremely boring, listening to his words of wisdom.

Half an hour into the inspection, the inspector came in with a small tin of *paan masala* and placed it reverentially near the DIG. He got an approving look. This was a new thing happening before me. The DIG opened the lid of the tin, found a small plastic spoon inside, scooped up a spoonful of that stuff and threw it into his mouth.

After about a minute or so, I jumped, startled, as I heard a loud, "Coook!" It sounded like the mating call of a huge bird. The sound had come from the DIG. Before I could gather my wits, there was another, feebler "Coook!"

It seemed that the stuff had produced some instant reaction in the system of the DIG, which was manifesting in the form of violent hiccups. These mating calls continued, though their frequency and intensity kept decreasing. After about thirty minutes, the calls stopped. It was time for the DIG to open the lid again and scoop up another dose of that stuff.

"Coook!" This loud call was followed by gradual low-intensity calls for another thirty minutes.

After consuming about seven spoonfuls of the stimulating stuff, the inspection was completed. The DIG's face was flushed from the effects of the *masala*. He gave me a look, which more or less conveyed, 'See? This is how an inspection has to be done.'

I had no intention of debating over unspoken words and just smiled back.

***

Around this time, the country was passing through a difficult period. Terrorism in Punjab was a cause of concern for everyone. The effects of this were even seen in Delhi, where a series of low-intensity explosions were happening. Transistor radios, fitted with some kind of improvised explosive devices, were placed in crowded areas. As someone unsuspecting would pick them up and switch them on, they would explode.

There was panic all around. Rourkela being an industrial city, we were keeping a keen watch. To our misfortune, one morning, I got a call from a police station. An unidentified bag had been found placed near a *paan* shop close to the railway station. It was an urgent matter of concern and I felt that it should be brought to the knowledge of the DIG immediately.

I called him and told him the news. There was complete silence from his end.

"Hello, hello!" I shouted. All I could hear was some deep breathing. I thought that the information must have stunned him. "Hello," I said again.

"I am coming to the police station," he said.

There was an emergency meeting, chaired by him, at the police station.

"Have you requisitioned the bomb squad?" he asked me.

"Yes, Sir. The earliest they can come is by tomorrow."

"Tomorrow?"

"Yes, Sir. They have to come from Ranchi."

Those days, we had to depend on the army for the disposal of bombs and explosives.

"Then we have to evacuate the area. Get me a map of that area."

"Map? We don't have any maps," I blurted out.

"No maps?"

"No, Sir."

By then, a clever sub-inspector had drawn a sketch of the area and passed it over to me.

"We have a sketch."

I handed it over to the DIG.

"Oh!" Now, he had something to work on. He took a pencil and drew a circle around the spot where the bag had been found.

"The area around a hundred feet radius of this circle has to be evacuated."

It was one of the most crowded areas of Rourkela. The circle he had marked covered a wide area and included a big hotel, a cinema hall and many houses.

"Evacuation will be a difficult task. Shouldn't we try to move the bag?" I suggested.

"Move the bag? Move the bag?" He repeated it for effect. "Don't you know? If you even touch it, it will explode."

"Explode?"

"Yes. You don't have any knowledge about this matter."

I kept quiet. Perhaps after his explosive affair with the commode, he was better prepared to deal with explosions.

"If you can't evacuate the area, it has to be protected by sandbags all around to a height of at least 4 feet."

"From where will we get so many sandbags?"

"Contact the executive engineer, PWD."

The engineer was contacted.

He said, "I will provide you with as many empty bags as you need, but you have to go to the river bed, fill sand in them and carry them back for your use."

With this information, immediate encircling of the area with sandbags was ruled out. The DIG was in a quandary. All his solutions to contain an imminent explosion were coming to nought, but he had to say something. An officer of his experience could not be found wanting in ideas.

"Then let us stop all movement of men and vehicles in the area. Declare it as a no-man zone."

The implementation of his latest idea would have created panic. We could not possibly prevent people from having access to the railway station. Instead of arguing with him, I went to another room, called up the police headquarters and briefed the Special DG about the situation.

"Why don't you somehow remove the bag?" he suggested.

"The DIG feels that it will immediately explode."

"Oh! Then why don't you try to hook it with something long and carry it?"

"We will try, Sir."

I called the inspector and discussed the matter. It was decided that we should get a long, stout bamboo and hook it to the handle of the bag. While this strategy was being worked out, the DIG was becoming restive in the other room. He summoned us and enquired as to what was happening.

"We are making preparations for enforcing the no-man area."

"Good. You must go personally and see to it."

"Yes, Sir." It was a good opportunity for us to leave.

At the site, the bamboo had arrived. It was delicately pushed into the handle of the bag and the bag lifted. Nothing happened. Emboldened by this, we decided to push the bamboo through so that the handle of the bag was in the middle of the bamboo. It would be easy to carry the bag away with two persons holding the bamboo at either end and the bag dangling in the middle.

Our aim was to somehow take the bag away from this crowded locality. The plan conceived was to engage two motorcycles. The pillion riders would hold the two ends of the bamboo and move about three kilometres to a secluded spot used for dumping the steel plant slag.

Unfortunately, at this stage, the DIG arrived. He got down from his car and on seeing the bag dangling from the bamboo, he shrieked, "Eeeeeiiiiii!" He rushed back to his car, shouting, "There is a difference between being brave and foolhardy."

No one responded, but in that commotion, I could catch words like 'fools', 'idiots' and the like coming from the car.

The motorcyclists positioned themselves and the bamboo was held from both sides. The motorcycles started moving.

The DIG started screaming, "The ignition of the motorcycle engines can also cause the bomb to explode." Thinking that the explosion was now imminent, he rushed off from the scene.

The bag was taken to the decided spot. There was a water body nearby. I suggested that the bag could be placed inside the water, but one officer was keen to put an end to this horrible affair.

He got a new sharp blade. Since the bag was made of Rexine, he cut out a portion of it from the side. What we found inside made us all burst into a fit of laughter.

There was a bundle of aluminium wire in the bag. It seemed some petty thief must have cut that piece of wire and stuffed it into the bag. To avoid being caught, he had possibly left it there to collect it later.

I reported the matter first to the Special DG and then called the DIG. He had left the scene, screaming.

"Okay," was all that he said.

Fortunately, the adjectives that were so liberally used by him an hour earlier, questioning our mental capabilities, were kept on hold.

***

One day, we had a case of a bank robbery. It was quite a daring act. Four persons entered the bank with their faces covered and soon after, brandished some weapons that they were carrying. The bank staff, not accustomed to such behaviour, simply panicked. They were ordered by these miscreants to hand over the cash. Having got around four to five lakhs of cash, they left the bank, walked back to their waiting vehicle and left the spot.

This was quite a sensational case for us. Since it happened in broad daylight in a busy street of the city and the money looted was a very big amount in those days, it posed a serious challenge for us.

We reached the spot and tried to elicit as much information as possible from the shaken bank employees. A team was deployed to talk to people in the area and gather information about the getaway vehicle. While this was in progress, the DIG, who was informed of the matter, summoned all of us immediately to his office.

This was rather odd. There was no time to hold meetings. However, we had no choice. Leaving some officers behind to pursue the matter, we went to the DIG's office.

He was well-prepared to conduct the meeting. A map was spread out in front of him and he was studying it intently. He had a strong conviction that a map is an essential requirement for police work. Without even finding out what had transpired and what information we had collected, he plunged in and took control straight away.

"Prepare four teams," he ordered. "Each team should comprise five armed men and be led by a sergeant." Then he marked four points on the map, each in different directions. "They should proceed to these points immediately and reach within half an hour."

"Sir, the points you have marked are far off. The teams will take at least two hours to reach them, if not more."

"What? You have no idea. See, they are so close by."

"They appear to be close on a map, but the actual distance is much more."

"You don't seem to know much about maps. One inch in the map is equivalent to one mile. These places are only two inches away."

"Sir, you are referring to the one-inch maps or topo sheets. This one in front of you is not a topo sheet."

"What?"

"Sir, please check the scale below. It says 'One inch is equal to 50 kilometres.'"

"Oh! But in any case, let them go."

"What will they do there?"

"They will move around and collect information and check suspicious activities."

"Sir, do you think armed men will be good for this kind of job?"

"Don't argue. They should proceed at once. Now, let us discuss the modus operandi."

He went on and on, depriving us of precious time to organise a proper investigation.

On returning, I discussed the matter with the Additional SP.

"This man will not let us work in peace."

"Sir, we have to devise some way to put an end to this."

After a couple of months, another crime took place, though not of the earlier magnitude. Promptly, a call came from the DIG, summoning us to report to his office for a meeting.

This time, both the Additional SP and I were well-prepared. Each of us carried a notebook with the names of suspects and criminals involved in various cases in the district. The moment the DIG started the meeting, both of us totally ignored him. We opened our respective notebooks and flipped the pages. He was keenly watching us.

"Padhi *Babu*," I said to the Additional SP.

"Yes, Sir."

"To me, it seems the work of Albert Dung Dung."

Padhi *Babu* looked at me, pondered for some time, looked at his notebook and responded, "Yes, Sir, but it could be Christopher Tirkey as well. He has a similar modus."

"Right," I agreed.

The DIG, we could see, was looking at both of us with a gaping mouth. He was totally perplexed. Both of us continued our discussion, exchanging more names and their locations, while paying no heed to the DIG, who, by now, had a totally dejected look on his face. We could see his frustration as he could not refer to his map and give directions as he had done earlier. This time, we had moved up by several notches with specifics. He was not prepared with any names.

"We have to check the movements of Michael Lobo as well."

"Lobo?" The DIG interjected. "Lobo is a Goanese name."

He was closely following our conversation and probably, writing down the names, too.

"Oh! Did I say Lobo? Sorry, I meant Michael Xess."

"Xess?"

"Yes, Sir. Michael Xess is a notorious criminal from the Manoharpur area," Padhi supplemented.

This confirmation totally deflated the DIG. Whatever little chance he had to catch me out had now vanished.

"Okay, you seem to have done a good study of the matter. See that you catch the criminals involved."

"Yes, Sir." We departed.

He stopped calling us for any more meetings.

***

A most unfortunate event, the assassination of the Prime Minister, shook the entire country. Many cities were affected by a backlash against a particular community. Events happened so suddenly that in the initial stages, we were unable to anticipate and formulate strategies to deal with the situation.

On the first day, nothing serious happened, but photographs of the late leader were placed at various points in busy market areas and people converged there. Soon, these small groups, numbering between fifteen and twenty, started raising slogans and were becoming unruly. We were in the process of engaging them in discussion and requesting them to move out so that normal life and traffic could be restored.

At this stage, I found the DIG arriving at the main market in his car. On occasions when he had to arrive at places where some law and order issues were involved, he had the habit of bringing a few armed personnel in his car, one in the front seat and two on either side of him in the back seat. It was quite a sight. Only he knew how he felt comfortable with this kind of seating arrangement in the car.

On reaching the spot, the guards and the DIG alighted and surveyed the scene. Suddenly, I don't know what got into him for he took out the whistle from the chest pocket of his uniform, put it into his mouth, started whistling at full blast and ran.

Seeing this, the three guards also started running behind him. To see four people in uniform, running and whistling, was quite perplexing, more so for the onlookers and the small groups that had gathered. They perhaps thought that something terrible was about to happen. Everyone started running away.

After completing his first run and being satisfied with the result, the DIG came towards where we were standing. It was my turn to look at him with a gaping mouth.

"You see, this is called an unofficial curfew."

He seemed to be mighty pleased seeing people running away. Then he saw another group assembling at a distance. He simply dashed off, whistling loudly. His guards followed him. I stood there stupefied, just watching the unfolding scene. Having scattered the group, he stopped and saw some people at the other end. The running and whistling resumed.

These shuttle runs continued for some time and I could see that he was getting tired. After all, the DIG was not known for his athletic prowess. He must have also realised that the unofficial curfew was not lasting for too long and his tactics needed a re-look. He left the scene. We had to use all our persuasive skills in convincing the groups to take away the photographs and leave the place.

By the second and third days, the situation was becoming more tense. Families belonging to the particular community were being targeted and attacked. However, our patrol vehicles could reach in time to avert any major incidents. We decided to start moving all these families to one place where they could be properly protected.

Once this was done, a new problem surfaced. The houses vacated were targeted by miscreants and set on fire by breaking the windows. The DIG had decided to leave his office and was permanently in one of the police stations, which was the closest to the market and the steel plant.

Everyone was busy and almost all the staff were moving around in their localities. The police station was more or less deserted, except for one or two staff members, the DIG and his guards. The fire station was also located inside this police station premises. As the number of incidents of arson increased, the fire station became very busy.

Every ten to fifteen minutes, a fire engine would start ringing its bell. Every time the bell rang, the DIG would come out of his room, totally dishevelled, look sadly at the passing engine and go back to his room. It was a sad sight. He had gone into a state of depression and was perhaps convinced that it was the beginning of an apocalypse.

I, along with the additional district magistrate, were spending most of our time in our car, moving around all over the city throughout the day and night. One evening, we entered that particular police station and found it totally deserted. What intrigued us was that even the DIG and his guards were missing. Finally, someone appeared, and we enquired as to what had happened and the whereabouts of the DIG.

The man was in a state of shock and replied, "There has been a firing."

"Firing?" We both shouted.

"Where?"

"Near the traffic gate."

"Where is the DIG?"

"He has gone to the spot."

We rushed to that place, which was quite close. The area was dimly lit and we could see no one. We looked around for some time and finally, we saw the DIG's car parked. We reached the spot and found an inspector there. We enquired from him as to what had happened.

One family of the community had preferred to stay in their house. In the evening, a group of miscreants had converged near the house. On seeing them, an inmate fired one round from his licensed gun, which scared the miscreants and they ran away. This was about all.

At this stage, the DIG emerged from somewhere, looking very concerned. On seeing us, he said grimly, "Now, firings have started."

"What firing, Sir? The man fired in self-defence. It is a good thing."

He had neither the energy nor the inclination to argue. The picture of an apocalypse was firmly set in his mind.

As we were about to start from there, a new problem arose. It was found that the DIG's driver was missing. Everyone present looked around the area and shouted his name, but there was no response.

The DIG was looking forlorn. He took out his whistle. I thought that he would start running again, but this time, he stood there and blew his whistle. It was not the shrill whistling that had accompanied his sprints, but one in a very low frequency, sounding quite melancholic.

After three to four low-frequency melancholic calls, the driver emerged from the darkness. He could not ignore his master's desperate call and seemed well-tuned to that frequency. I realised at that moment that here was a police officer who knew the effective use of a whistle. I wanted to ask him where he had learnt these different types of calls but decided that it was not the right time.

There was no apocalypse. The riots ended in another couple of days and we could bring about normalcy.

Time passed and soon, it was time for the general elections. Busy days started again, with extensive police arrangements, mobilisation of manpower, briefing sessions and the like. Complaints and counter-complaints from various political parties were received, and we had to look into each case with utmost impartiality.

The day of polling drew nearer and tension increased. Finally, the time came for propaganda to stop forty-eight hours prior to polling. As we were preparing for parties to be dispatched to various booths, an alarming call came, informing us about serious tension in a particular area.

I, along with others, rushed to the spot and was stunned by what we saw there. We found the DIG's car, blocked by an irate mob, shouting and abusing. A sub-inspector was trying his best to clear the road but could not succeed due to the abusive crowd. As a result, he was indulging in what could be best described as jumping on the spot.

His action was further infuriating the crowd. We ran towards the car. On seeing us, the sub-inspector stopped jumping and sheepishly informed us that the DIG had been detained and he was trying to clear the road. The DIG and his guards were inside the car and showed no inclination to come out of it.

As soon as we cleared the road, the DIG sped off from the scene without even looking back at us. We found out that the DIG had accompanied the ruling party candidate to the area during the no-propaganda period. This was not taken well by the supporters of the other party and they had stopped the DIG's car and were demanding an explanation from him. Somehow, they were pacified, and we left.

The DIG never raised this subject with me. The elections ended, results were declared and the ruling party candidate lost.

I was immediately transferred out. The DIG remained there. Fortunately for me, my days with Mr Fidgety were over.

# The Orangutan

"Zäo shang häo," the Chinese general greeted the director with a broad smile as soon as he entered his office and parked himself in a chair.

The director had been informed about the visit of the general and was expecting him in his office. On seeing the well-built general, he appeared a bit taken aback but managed to flash his best smile. After all, the visit had to pass off smoothly.

However, on hearing these words of greeting, the generous smile on the director's face started fading. Faced with something which was not anticipated, his eyebrows shot up and he appeared confused. Before he could think of what to do, the general further confounded him, saying, "Wö hěn róngxìng cānguān guì xiào."

The director sat dumbfounded. His eyebrows returned to their normal position, but his jaw dropped, giving him a gaping look. Not knowing what to say or do, he looked around and saw me. *What have you got me into?* I could read his thoughts from the expression on his face.

Before I could say something, the interpreter took over, "Good morning. It is my privilege to visit your academy."

The director quickly turned his head and looked at the interpreter. His face lit up. The smile was back on his face and he looked absolutely thrilled. I had a strong feeling that he wanted to stand up and hug the interpreter. Luckily, even if he had the urge to do so, he controlled himself very well but gave way to a strange sound, "Ooooo!"

It was a long sound, lasting for about ten seconds. It was not Chinese or even English but a spontaneous outpour of relief. The interpreter had made him realise that the matter was not as complicated as he had thought.

Thereafter, the conversation between the Chinese general and our director, through the interpreter, went ahead with great bonhomie. They never gave a chance to anyone else to join in. After a long chat, it was decided that they would take a tour of the academy. By the end of the visit, the two of them had become so friendly that the Chinese general had Paan Parag offered to him.

This was Mr Das, the director. He was a man with a cherubic personality, fun-loving but totally committed to the work at hand. 'Oooooo' seemed to be his favourite oral expression. He would utter it while expressing relief, pain, pleasure or even approval. The mode of utterance differed in each case, and one had to have a fine listening ability to detect the difference.

Once, a senior faculty member went into his chamber for some work. He entered the room, saluted him and settled down in a chair. Soon thereafter, he started speaking about the issue for which he had come. Mr Das was watching him keenly. Once the faculty member stopped speaking, Mr Das looked at him and said, "You come in, straight away sit on a chair and start off with your problem. What is this?"

The perplexed officer looked at him and could not understand what to say.

Mr Das continued, "In our times, when we used to go to a senior officer, we used to stand in front of him, trembling and sweating. Taking a seat was simply out of the question. You just come in and settle down comfortably?"

By then, the officer had gathered his wits. He looked at Mr Das seriously and explained, "Sir, you would not know. When we come to you, we stand outside your door, sweating and take a few minutes just to muster the courage to come inside. Then we wipe our faces and start thinking of what to say when we are face to face with you. Having done this, we come inside and try to finish our work as early as possible and go back."

Mr Das looked at him with a big smile and said, "Ooooooowww!"

This 'Oooooowww' conveyed absolute bliss. It sounded like a cat purring when stroked lovingly by its master. The realisation that he also was as feared as any of the old-time officers gave him a feeling of intense pleasure.

Mr Das would take a lot of interest in training. Every morning, he came out, dressed in shorts, with a baton in his hand and moved around in the campus. He would invariably come into the parade ground to watch the trainees doing their morning outdoor activities. He made it a habit to enter classrooms and sit quietly, listening to the lectures and assessing their quality.

One day, he went into a classroom where a guest lecturer was addressing the trainees. He quietly parked himself near the head table. The lecturer was moving around and passionately explaining something. The director was listening to him intently. At this stage, the prevailing peace was considerably shattered as the guest lecturer decided to come and sit on the head table with his back to the director. Mr Das got up and left the room in a huff.

The next day, in the staff meeting, he appeared glum.

"What kind of people do you invite as guest faculty?" Before anyone could say anything, he continued, "Yesterday, that idiot came and sat in front of me on the table."

"Oh!" someone blurted out.

"All I could see was his posterior. That man does not even have basic manners. How will he teach? I had a great desire to stand up and give him a good kick on his posterior, but I controlled myself."

Having announced his desire, he felt a little relieved and was back to his normal self. He had sent out the message loud and clear that he could take strong physical action if necessary. After all, he believed in old-time values. No one dared to show him his posterior.

He was a fun-loving man, who loved his drinks and enjoyed music. He used to enjoy parties. There used to be a party almost every week.

A party was organised for retired senior officers on the completion of 50 years since they joined the service. Mr Das was at his best, showing them around and playing the role of the perfect host.

The elderly gentlemen were quite touched by his warmth and attention. As the party progressed, Mr Das had his regular quota of drinks and was enjoying the party. We saw him offering a few of the gentlemen a lift in his car to their guest houses.

The next morning, we saw him in a rather glum mood.

On being questioned, he said, "These oldies really spoilt my evening. It was such a lovely party, but all the fun was lost."

"What happened, Sir?"

"*Arre,* I was foolish to have offered them a lift. One of them was totally obsessed with the water jet in his commode."

"Commode?"

"Yes, he felt that the jet was not spraying in the right direction. He dragged me to his toilet and showed me that thing."

"That's terrible, Sir."

"*Kya* terrible, he spoilt all the fun. Just imagine, after those lovely drinks, going and seeing a commode. Am I a plumber?" he questioned. "One should maintain a good distance from these people."

The journey with him in the academy, though short, was extremely pleasant, with such small incidents adding spice to the otherwise bland routine. He was always available and was present at all events, including the movie time at the auditorium, taking part in games and sports, listening to debates and elocution competitions and giving his views on everything.

He would visit faculty members with his wife and interact with them socially. He would call the trainees home so that they could pick up the nuances of calling on seniors. On the whole, he was one person who was actually cut out for that role. He automatically earned the respect and position of the head of the family of that small group of officers.

A good run cannot continue forever. There is a fair chance that you will meet a hurdle sooner than expected. The same applies to one's service career, too. There is always a strong possibility of having a worthless person as your boss. This catastrophic possibility did not spare me. It happened at a most unexpected time.

Mr Das completed his long innings in the service and had to leave on attaining the age of superannuation. We missed him and his lively nature a lot.

There was a gap of a few months with no director in the academy. Finally, we got news of the posting of a new officer. I had met him earlier but was not too familiar with his ways. One fine day or should I call it a fateful day, we welcomed Mr Phool Chand, the new director, to the academy.

Phool Chand stood out for his unique abilities. He was a police officer with virtually no experience of real policing. He had spent most of his days in non-police work after a stint with an intelligence agency. I had serious doubts about whether he had done anything useful in the agency also, for his initial days in the academy clearly indicated that the only expertise he had developed was to write something and then go on correcting it throughout the day.

Since the process involved active use of his brain power, he had developed a habit of stimulating it with a constant flow of nicotine. As a result, he gave the impression of a chimney billowing smoke all the time.

Since he had not worked in the regular police, he had hardly used his uniform. However, once one was in uniform, one had to follow some accepted practices, like saluting and receiving a salute, walking smartly and developing a pleasant countenance.

Phool Chand made earnest efforts to learn these skills. He saluted at good speed but was unable to control his hand once it had reached the saluting position. It kept shaking like a tuning fork for some time before settling down. His attempt to walk smartly met with more disastrous results. He had a funny gait, with his posterior somewhat jutting out. This was often seen in a few freshers and every batch in the academy had heard the instructors shouting, "Don't walk like a pregnant duck" at trainees with this kind of gait.

With constant goading, they improved, but who was to teach the director? In uniform, he probably became more conscious and to make his walk look smart, he pushed his posterior further, making him look like a duck in a very advanced stage of pregnancy.

Waking up early was part of the academy routine. For us, the day started around 5 in the morning. Phool Chand turned out to be one who had perhaps developed an aversion to the morning sun quite early in life. The adage, 'the early bird catches the worm', held no meaning for him. Why would he bother with worms when the late-night owl got all the drinks?

When he appeared for the day at 10 in the morning, he would look bleary-eyed. Possibly, he was being deprived of precious sleep. With this kind of habit, he had no clue about the outdoor activities of the trainees. To make up for this lapse, he decided to start an outdoor activity. He chose to ride and that too in the afternoon.

Mr Das was a clever man and had avoided any contact with the equine species during his stay. There were, of course, a few directors, who being fine riders during their times, had taken to riding and used to come to the parade ground majestically on horseback in the morning. Phool Chand did not look like one who could even sit properly on a horse, let alone ride it majestically.

The fact that he chose to ride confirmed that he was a person who had never taken his outdoor classes seriously as a trainee and had avoided the equestrian classes on some pretext. Once a trainee takes part in the equestrian classes, he learns about the various incidents, episodes and disasters involving horses.

Horses are benign animals but have their own moods and tantrums. I am convinced that they derive great pleasure in unsettling a rider and do things as per their will.

Knowing this, would any sensible man choose to go near them and that too at such a late stage in his life? Phool Chand had certainly avoided the riding classes during his training and hence, was unaware of the dangers that lurked.

He appeared one day in his new breeches and helmet. The riding staff, most reverentially, attended to him. They could assess his ability from his gait and demeanour. The most docile horse, advanced in age and about to retire, was chosen for him. Phool Chand was made to mount and taken on a slow walk, with a syce leading the horse, holding his reins. This continued for a couple of days.

Phool Chand seemed to be quite happy with his progress. On the third or fourth day, while ambling along, the horse suddenly made a sound, which sounded like, "Bhurrrrrrr."

Though startled, Phool Chand did not react much and continued with his journey. The horse decided to let out a second 'Bhurrrrrrrrr' with greater intensity, followed by a perceptible increase in his speed. The combination of a stronger 'Bhurrrrrr' and the change of speed affected Phool Chand terribly.

He let out a scream and was preparing to jump off the horse when he was persuaded not to do so. The syce was severely admonished for failing to discipline the horse. The riding-in-charge rushed to the spot and somehow convinced the director that for his safety, a second syce on the other side of the horse could be introduced.

Thereafter, Phool Chand was led by two persons, one on either side of the horse. This arrangement continued to the satisfaction of all parties for a few days, but after all, a horse is a horse and has its own will and moods.

One day, while the procession was moving slowly, a problem of high intensity originated from the rear unguarded side of the horse. Possibly being tripped by a stone, the horse bucked, raising his hind part and rushed forward. Phool Chand was badly unsettled. A cold chill ran down his spine. Even a strong person gets unnerved by an unexpected sound or threat from behind. Phool Chand, on horseback, was in a state of reasonably high tension.

This sudden up and forward movement in close succession was a bit too much for him. He was so stunned that he could neither scream nor shout; instead, he let go of a pathetic yelp and was shaking with fright. Everyone rushed to the spot and a thorough evaluation of this disaster was carried out.

To restore the confidence level of the director, two more syces were introduced to guard the rear part of the horse. Guarded by four syces, Phool Chand's equestrian practice continued but not for long. It was not very clear as to why it ended. One version was that Phool Chand gave up. He realised that with this kind of arrangement, he would never be able to make his dramatic entry into the parade ground.

It was also rumoured that the riding staff politely told him that his riding with four people guarding him would send a wrong message to the trainees. Though he gave up riding and visits to the riding ground, he had developed a great love for the riding attire. In the afternoons, he would be invariably seen in breeches and a t-shirt.

Not knowing the ways of the academy and having been totally unconnected with police work for a long time proved to be extremely mortifying for Phool Chand at times. His choice of uniform in the afternoon exposed him to the first such embarrassment. He was smoking contentedly in the comfort of his room one afternoon, dressed in his breeches, when the deputy director came in and told him that he had to attend the inauguration of a volleyball inter-squad tournament.

Though he had no intention of attending this rather tedious event, he could not refuse to go. He got up and accompanied the deputy director with a cigarette in his hand. As they were proceeding towards the ground, the deputy director looked at him closely and said, "Sir, I think you are not in the proper attire."

Phool Chand was affronted by this remark. He had never been told so by any of his subordinates. However, having no clue as to the reason for the deputy director's observation, he controlled himself and asked, "What is wrong with my attire?"

"Sir, you are in breeches, which is the riding uniform. It is not complete without the headgear."

"Headgear?"

"Yes, Sir. You have to put on your helmet."

"You mean I have to put on the helmet in this hot sun?"

"Having come in breeches, I am afraid you have no choice, Sir."

Phool Chand threw his cigarette away and rushed back to his room. He emerged a while later with his helmet on his head and looking like some kind of supervisor at a construction site. The deputy director was proving to be difficult for him to handle. Phool Chand must have made up his mind to act in the most proper manner to not give the deputy director another chance to find fault with him.

They reached the games area where everyone was in sports attire with no headgear. If one is in sports dress, the usual way to salute is to just come to attention. Phool Chand was in a peculiar situation. He had to stand up and salute. He was so affected by the helmet incident that whenever he saw some trainee coming close to attention, even while playing, he would get up and salute.

The evening turned out to be a miserable one. Finally, the ordeal was over and Phool Chand returned to the comfort of his own room. Having charged his system adequately with nicotine and caffeine, he got back to his favourite work of writing rubbish and correcting it.

While engaged in this, he also made up his mind to give up his favourite attire, the breeches. From then on, he was seen in white shorts and shirt. He could no longer bear the indignity of standing up and saluting and that too, while wearing a helmet.

Alas! This was not the end of his woes. Another incident, which he had least anticipated, happened soon afterwards in the forenoon session when Phool Chand was dressed in the regular uniform. The same deputy director came into his room and requested him to accompany him to watch the trainees perform an activity called unarmed combat.

This time, Phool Chand appeared confident in handling the situation as he was in a proper dress as the others. They went to the gymnasium hall where the event was taking place. On entering the hall, Phool Chand noticed that the trainees and instructors were dressed differently in white judo robes.

He was taken aback and a bit apprehensive. The instructor, on seeing him, ordered the class to attention and came running towards the director to report. The moment he saw the instructor coming, Phool Chand froze and stood still. As the instructor reached and stood before him, Phool Chand thought it appropriate to raise his hand in salute.

When one is in judo robes, the tradition is to bow as a mark of respect. The instructor followed this and reverentially bowed. Phool Chand was thoroughly confused. He had not anticipated such a complex issue. Not knowing what to do, he quickly bowed, while still saluting.

Having bowed, he had no clue as to when he should return to the upright posture. Not wanting to be outdone in exchanging such courtesies, he remained in the bent posture for a good fifteen seconds more than the instructor. When, with a great feeling of accomplishment, he finally rose, he looked around to find people desperately trying to suppress their laughter.

It would be wrong to say that these incidents did not impact him. However, he was unable to find out what was wrong. He desperately wanted to avoid all these embarrassments. One solution that came to his mind was to be away from the academy. He had exalted notions about himself. After all, he was meant for bigger roles and should not have to waste his time bothering about salutes, parades and horses.

He set his sights on higher goals. He organised regular trips to Delhi, met people who mattered and gave them weird ideas about what he could do. Initially, they took him seriously, but it did not take them long to realise that he was just blabbering. To keep him at bay, they would agree to some project he suggested and send him off.

He would come rushing back to the academy, all charged up and start working on his grand ideas. These ideas, after being put on paper, went through a long process of refinement by way of several readings and corrections. Faculty members would be roped in to assist him in this task at the expense of their important work of preparing for classes.

After weeks of incessant writing, corrections and re-writing, the final product would be churned out. It would look no different from the one he had dictated in the first instance. Even so, he would look mighty pleased. He would rush off again to Delhi with the material and take days to discuss the matter.

With whom he discussed such matters was never made public. I had a sneaking suspicion that his great pieces of work were going straight into the shredder, but he never gave up. After all, this was all he knew.

The academy could be an unrelenting place. Despite Phool Chand's best efforts to stay away from the outdoors, there were occasions that required his presence as the head of the academy. One such event was the Police Martyrs' Day wreath-laying ceremony. All trainees, faculty and instructors line up on this occasion to pay homage to the fallen martyrs.

The practice was that every officer would go by turn, place a wreath and then return to his place. As the director, Phool Chand was to go first. When one goes to place the wreath, it has to be in a slow march with hands kept close to the body. With his jutting posterior, this walk in slow motion with hands kept tightly by his side was a bit of an issue for Phool Chand.

As soon as he started walking, his hands moved sideways, and he brought them back to position. This movement was constantly repeated, and the spectacle continued for as long as he was in the slow-motion march. His movements resembled those of a huge bird trying to take off but unable to do so because of some defect in his wings. Finally, the bird reached the memorial, but he was so drained, both physically and mentally, after this agonising walk that he forgot to salute. He quickly placed the wreath and came back to his place. The sniggers coming from the trainees were quite perceptible.

An imposing statue of Sardar Patel stands on a huge rock inside the academy. Over the years, the birth anniversary of the great leader has been celebrated with solemnity. Like the evolution of mankind, this function has also evolved over the years and gained in complexity.

I had heard that, in the initial days, only flowers were offered at the statue. Then someone thought of a garland. Since placing a garland on a huge statue during a function was simply not possible as no one could reach the top, it was decided that the exercise could be completed before the function started, using bamboo. The senior faculty members used to go to the already garlanded statue and offer flowers.

This continued for some time before someone thought of introducing the trainees to the ceremony. They were made to stand on the road in front of the statue and witness the function. Some directors thought that it was a fitting occasion to deliver a motivating speech. Hence, a speech by the director was introduced.

After his disastrous experience in the wreath-laying ceremony, Phool Chand had rushed off to Delhi. He had just returned and was trying to come up with ideas for a new project when the deputy director came into his room and told him about the birth anniversary of the great leader. He also briefed him about the latest format of the function.

This was quite a problem for Phool Chand as he had never anticipated another exposure to the outdoors so soon.

He queried, “Is it necessary for me to go?”

"Absolutely, Sir."

The deputy director was proving to be a bit of a nuisance for Phool Chand.

"Okay. There is no slow march in this, I suppose?"

"No, Sir."

"Good."

"Sir, you have to just climb the steps up to the statue and place the flowers, stand by the side and deliver your speech."

"Fine."

"Shall I prepare a draft speech for you, Sir?"

"No, no! I will do it."

How could he trust these outdoor types for the cerebral kind of work?

Phool Chand appeared on time for the function. The trainees and other faculty members had already lined up on the road. The deputy director came and reported to him and sought his permission to start the proceedings. Having got Phool Chand's approval, he marched towards the steps and the director followed him.

Not to be found wanting in his marching technique, Phool Chand ensured that his hands followed the proper upward and downward swing. He gloriously marched towards the steps, swinging his hands. Climbing steps while marching increases the difficulty level manifold. Generally, people climb up with normal movements, without paying much attention to the swing.

However, Phool Chand was determined to prove a point. As he started climbing, his leg movements became slower, but he kept up the hand swing. As a result, we could see a terrible mismatch in the hand-leg movement. The higher he climbed, the slower his legs became and to make up for this loss of speed, he swung his arms with greater fervour.

He wanted all possible power in his arms, with the fond hope that it would help him in his lift-off. At a particular point, the steps leading to the statue took a turn. He was not visible to us for a few seconds when he went behind in the turn, but when he emerged at the top, his hands were moving at frantic speed like the rotor of a helicopter.

He stopped at the statue, looking completely spent. His mouth was open and we could see him breathing heavily. It took him a couple of minutes to come back to normal. His efforts to impress the trainees with his spectacular arm movement had ended in a comical fiasco.

The academy posting was turning out to be somewhat of a misery for Phool Chand. He had never bargained for such barbaric procedures, especially when he was exposed to them. His only solace was the trips to Delhi and coming back with some projects, which kept him occupied. He made it a point to avoid all outdoor activities and decided to stick to his room.

As the days passed, the training schedule of the trainees also progressed. When the trainees were almost midway through their course, a rather unsavoury incident took place, which had a profound impact on the director.

A group of three trainees decided to go out for dinner at a roadside restaurant close to the campus. During dinner, the three could not resist the temptation of gulping down a few pegs of the stimulating brew, which was available on the sly in the restaurant. Having had their fill, they forgot all the woes of the hard physical training and were in a good mood.

It was felt that the mood could be further alleviated by smoking a few cigarettes. They reached a small cigarette shop and ordered their brand.

It is not clear as to what exactly happened after this, but an altercation started between the three and the shopkeeper either over the price or the change returned to them.

The initial response from both sides was restricted to verbal exchanges. The pitch and tenor of this means of communication slowly started increasing and after about five minutes, had reached dangerous decibel levels, attracting others to come and join in. The shopkeeper, being a local, had quite a few supporters.

The matter was getting complicated, but the trainees, still under the intoxicating effects of the drinks, were not able to judge the situation accurately. One of them, however, who was a little less intoxicated, could sense trouble and ran back to the campus to inform the others. The two who remained behind perhaps thought it appropriate to put the lessons on unarmed combat to good use.

First, they decided to warm up by making a few movements in the air. This provoked the opposite party to such an extent that they sprang up from their static positions and rushed towards the two. What followed was a free flow of blows and punches. The poor trainees, still under the effects of those drinks, were not able to direct their punches well.

In their anxiety to gain an upper hand, they had thrown caution to the winds and had left their faces exposed. Though not professional boxers, the other party took advantage of the situation and placed some powerful punches on the chin of one and a devastating blow on the nose of the other.

The fight was clearly becoming one-sided. Fortunately, before these two could be mauled any further, the third trainee had succeeded in his mission and come back with reinforcements. A large number of trainees arrived at the scene. On seeing them, the locals dispersed with great speed.

At this stage, news about the incident reached me. I, along with a few other faculty members, rushed to the place. We managed to send the trainees back. The injured trainees were sent to the hospital and the local police were informed of the matter.

Phool Chand was absent, and no one knew where he was. In the morning, he was informed about the whole affair. His supercilious behaviour on hearing about it stunned all of us.

"Oh ho," he said, displaying all his teeth. "So, your trainees are getting a bit thirsty, eh? Don't we have a bar here?"

"No, Sir."

"Oh! Call all the trainees at 4 pm. I would like to talk to them."

We came away, absolutely puzzled.

He came in at 4 pm with that big smile. Perhaps he wanted the trainees to be at ease.

"What is this affair of going to these roadside restaurants? You are officers. You must enjoy in a proper bar. After all, this place is known for good food and drinks."

Everyone was looking at him in utter disbelief, but he carried on. The trainees left, having been briefed that they should drink merrily.

However, after a couple of days, the scenario changed completely. Phool Chand looked as though he had been suddenly accosted by a ghost. His face resembled that of a crab and his body was shaking, either out of fright or a deep rage. His tone had changed when he announced in a gruff voice that serious cognisance was to be taken of the unruly conduct of the trainees. In fact, he had already written letters to the ministry, recommending action against the involved trainees.

That a person, who was so concerned about the thirst of the trainees just a couple of days ago, would do an about-turn so abruptly surprised us. We got to know that he had received a severe dressing-down from Delhi for mishandling the whole matter.

The cavalier attitude that he had displayed vanished instantly. He was a changed or rather, a deranged man after this. He held meeting after meeting to find out why discipline was on the decline but could not come up with any tangible solution.

He hit upon the idea that the comfort level of the trainees had been raised very high, as a result of which they were not being groomed the hard way. He decided to remove the air conditioners from the classrooms so that the trainees would learn to bear the heat along with the lectures. There was opposition to this idea, but he had made up his mind. He would now govern with an iron fist.

The iron-fisted rule continued. Faculty members, including me, who were, as per his understanding, close to the trainees, had to be closely watched. To enforce discipline, he had to sacrifice his frequent visits to Delhi and stuck to his room, writing reports.

It was now time for him to fetch some endorsement for the great work he had accomplished in putting the academy on the right track. He contacted Mr Khan, a former director and a person with a sterling reputation as an officer and trainer. He was invited to visit the academy.

Mr Khan arrived and was received with due courtesy. Phool Chand had made arrangements for Mr Khan to be briefed soon after his arrival and thereafter, taken to see the various measures he had implemented. The briefing or rather the small talk, was to take place in the club located next to the swimming pool.

Faculty members were asked to be present. All of us quietly settled down, and the stage was taken over by Phool Chand. He explained at length how he had been taking great interest in the training and that he personally took care of what inputs should go into lectures. He went on and on and finally, came to the issue of discipline.

"Sir, the trainees were becoming a bit soft."

"Why?"

"They were getting a lot of comfort compared to what we had during our training. They should know what hardship is."

Mr Khan kept quiet but was keenly listening to Phool Chand.

"Sir, they had air conditioners in the classrooms. To ensure that they learn what hard life is, I had all the air conditioners removed."

He thought he had scored a point.

Mr Khan looked at Phool Chand in disbelief and kept quiet for some time, perhaps trying to gather his thoughts. Then he looked Phool Chand straight in the eye and said rather sternly, "In this day and age, anyone who can even think of taking such retrograde steps is like an orangutan."

There was pin-drop silence for a few minutes. Phool Chand looked stunned and had a gaping look on his face. I observed him closely and he, indeed, appeared like an orangutan, one whose banana had been snatched away. My respect for Mr Khan went up several notches. Just in one meeting, he could sum up Phool Chand with such perfection.

Phool Chand was devastated, to say the least. Mr Khan's further programmes were left to the deputy director.

A few months later, I left the academy on the recommendation of the orangutan. He had been somehow convinced that I had had a hand in most of his problems.

# The Uncanny Boss

"You think I am a moron?" he croaked.

Where was the question of thinking when I was pretty much convinced about his mental abilities? However, discretion being the better part of valour, I preferred to let that question be.

We had lost a young and courageous officer, killed by the Naxals in a district bordering Jharkhand. His mortal remains had reached his home. The chief had been requested to come and lay a wreath. A police guard had been stationed for the last salute.

The boss arrived and started acting in a manner, which certainly could not be categorised as normal. He wandered all around the place. He would rush off to where he found a few people gathered together, indulge in small talk and then shoot off in another direction to meet yet another group. On a formal sombre occasion like this, one had to be very focused. However, that focus was nowhere to be seen in the chief.

After moving around for a long time, his gaze fell on the guard that had lined up near the body. He started walking towards them. It was at this stage that I felt I must intervene. I had a nagging suspicion that he might stand before them and expect a salute.

"Sir, the guard is for the martyr."

"You think I am a moron?" he shot back.

This was the person we had to deal with. I had heard a lot about him and was beginning to realise that it would be quite a task. Having come in contact with him for quite a few days by now, I had found that he had to be dependent on someone. He either lacked the confidence or the will to do things on his own.

Stories of his past – his days of frolic with friends, his pursuit of bliss through liberal use of spirits and fumes and his total dependence on his father for this rather weird and luxurious lifestyle – were flying thick and fast.

Someone, known to his father, had once narrated to me in detail how he had had to rush with a large sum of money to rescue this man along with his friends from a hotel where they had been held captive, being unable to clear the bill. An adult's dependence on pocket money is rather odd, but it takes all kinds to make the world. He happened to be one such specimen.

The transition from pocket money to public life and assuming the role of a mass leader may seem like some kind of fairy tale. One has read so many stories of fairy godmothers helping people achieve impossible tasks. For this man, the transition was no less dramatic. His fairy godmother was his late father's good deeds.

Being catapulted to a position of absolute power and eminence in a jiffy can be quite unnerving for anyone. How this development affected him is quite difficult to speculate, but as days passed, one thing that became more and more evident was his need to depend on someone who he could trust. He was simply incapable of comprehending matters and making decisions on his own.

This display of his rather childlike intellectual abilities, after assuming a high position in public life, baffled many. Once, while discussing important matters of the state, a senior bureaucrat in charge of agriculture volunteered some information to him.

"Sir, this year, the monsoon has been adequate."

This information rattled the boss quite a bit. After remaining silent for some time, he put his thought process into analysing this innocuous information. Perhaps, he was unable to make anything of it. With a look of concern and apprehension, he asked, "Is it good or bad?"

There was an interesting episode when he went on a visit to his area. A public meeting was organised where he was to interact with the local citizens. Being one who shunned direct interface with people, he had to be persuaded to attend it. He sat on the dais with a frown on his face, making not even the slightest attempt to hide his utter contempt for the large gathering in front of him.

As the meeting progressed, the local people became more and more interactive. They were freely venting their grievances and started raising many issues. This man had never expected this to happen. He had thought that his appearance would be enough and that he could just leave in a short while.

As the demands and questions became louder, his frown changed into a look of utter disgust. He was muttering something, which was not audible in that din. This was when he realised that he had to take control. He ordered in Hindi, "*MLA ko bulao* (Call the MLA)."

The persons nearby heard him. They looked at him in disbelief but preferred to keep quiet because he was the local MLA. Not getting any response to his order and seeing no change in the mood of the crowd, he again commanded and this time, rather sternly, "*MLA ko jaldi bulao* (Call the MLA quickly)."

His aides were quite perplexed, but one of them mustered the courage to go near him and whisper in his ear, "Sir, you are the local MLA."

Now, it was his turn to stare at the aide in utter disbelief. He realised that his escape route had been sealed. Soon, his look of disbelief turned into one of abject misery. His expression was like that of a puppy whose cookie had been suddenly snatched away from him. With this look, he almost pleaded with his men to somehow salvage the situation. While the people were waiting for their answers, he simply walked away. The organisers made some announcement about his busy schedule that required him to leave.

A great public leader indeed!

Before being chosen to be the boss in the state, he had shown his brilliance as a smaller boss in the federal set-up. One of the onerous responsibilities bestowed on him, as a smaller boss, was to answer questions in the legislature relating to his department.

This, we all know, can be quite a daunting task. One had to really prepare well, understanding the basic issues and making one's own fundamentals clear. Various people had different ways of preparation. I remember one rather promising classmate of ours who had taken this very seriously for our post-graduate examinations.

He had meticulously prepared an exhaustive question bank and thereafter, researched well and prepared answers for all of them. Having done this, he entered the most difficult phase of memorising the answers. After spending long hours and sleepless nights, he managed to learn by heart the answers to all the questions on his list.

He looked so well-prepared and oozed such confidence that we felt totally unprepared. Finally, the examinations started. After our first paper was over, I went up to him and found him very morose and depressed.

"What happened?" I asked.

He looked up at me, completely shattered.

"I couldn't answer all the questions," he replied.

"What?"

"Yes, I could complete only three of the five."

"But you were so well-prepared?"

"Yes, I knew all the answers but did not have enough time."

"Why?"

"You see, I had memorised all the answers in chronological order as per my question bank."

"Yes." I encouraged him to reveal further.

"But the questions in the examination were not in that order."

"So what?" I queried.

"So what?" He looked at me with some anger.

"But why couldn't you write the answers?"

"The first question in the question paper was number 4 on my list."

"So?"

"So, I was not able to recall the answer to number 4 immediately."

"Oh!"

"Yes, I had to start recalling the answers in my mind in the same order in which I had memorised them."

"Oh!" This time, my 'Oh' was a bit more emphatic and louder.

"You see, I had to spend considerable time getting the right answers to the questions."

"Very sad."

"I could complete only three. I knew all the answers, but time ran out."

He kept on mumbling to himself, "I knew all the answers, I knew all the answers." He was looking down and holding his head. I thought it was time for me to leave.

That was it. You can now realise that the process of answering questions is not all that easy. Various persons pass through different levels of difficulty. There can be all kinds of pitfalls.

Our great minister certainly had a task in hand. The process of answering questions in the legislature is quite different from doing so in an examination.

In the legislature, the initial question is written and comes well in advance. A proper reply is drafted and the smaller boss has to read it out. Thereafter, supplementary questions are asked, which are verbal and impromptu answers have to be given. This is where the difficulty level rises manifold.

To make things easy, a fairly simple method is followed. Officers acquainted with the subject position themselves in the adjoining gallery, armed with information. Whenever any question comes up, they promptly write down the answers and pass it on to the smaller boss who has to only read out the relevant answers.

There is not much memorising involved. The process looks quite organised and has been time-tested. However, for our smaller boss, things went terribly wrong and ended in a disaster.

On the appointed day, he proceeded to the legislature, properly briefed and with the answer to his question. When his turn came, he read out the answer with great elan. Then came the verbal supplementary questions. His aides in the official gallery had already provided him with a list of possible questions and their answers.

All he had to do was to find the relevant question from the list and read out its answer. This task proved too much for him. He shuffled through the papers and looked here and there. Since the answers were already provided to him, his aides could not do much. Seeing no other way, he finally read out the first answer on the sheet, which was not related to that supplementary question at all.

There was a hushed silence all around. Then came another question. The silence after his answer to the first question perhaps gave him the impression that he had fared very well. Hence, he followed the same procedure and read out another answer, which was unrelated to the second question. This time, all hell broke loose.

There was shouting and screaming in the legislature about the minister not knowing anything. In the din and commotion, the poor man was sheepishly looking here and there, searching for some clue as to what had gone wrong. Before he could find out the cause, the Speaker intervened and advised him to come better prepared.

The next day, the press was very harsh. What impact this had on the smaller boss is difficult to guess, but his political journey was not the least affected.

He was clever enough to make suitable arrangements to ensure that such a thing never happened again. On his joining the state, he and his advisors developed a somewhat peculiar method of circumventing the problem. Questions were also asked in the assembly and as a minister, he had to answer them.

Briefing sessions were organised to acquaint him with the answers and possible supplementaries. The officers who were supposed to brief him used to be well-prepared with all relevant data and figures. He would pretend to be all ears for a few minutes. Then his gaze would wander, first to his advisor on the right, then to the one on the left.

After gazing at them for a few minutes in turn, he would start grinning like a Cheshire cat. This was possibly some sort of secret signal. The senior advisor would politely say that they would be able to manage with the information already given and no further briefing would be necessary.

All would leave, wondering how he would be able to reply. Little were they aware of the finely worked-out method. On the day of the question-answer session, the questioner would invariably absent himself. If there is no questioner, the question is never asked and hence, no answer is required. This continued, and he never had to again undergo the torture that he had faced earlier. However, the briefings continued.

He learnt another important lesson from this misadventure. Never did he agree to meet anyone from the press for a briefing or impromptu talk. For him, impromptu was a synonym for disaster. His trusted team worked on back-channel communication with the press. Soon, he started getting rave reports about his capabilities and intentions. What transpired behind the scenes never came out in public but was not very difficult to guess.

The way he dressed was rather strange or maybe queer. Not much information could be gathered about what he wore in his pocket-money-dependence days. Some say he used to be attired in normal shirts and trousers. Nobody really cared to pay attention to him. It was only after he came into public life that people started noticing him.

He dressed himself in impeccable whites, a long *kurta* and pyjamas. His footwear was a pair of *chappals*. The *kurta* was loose enough to hide the contours of his body, which kept increasing in girth to match the rather fast rate at which his stomach was growing. The length of the pyjamas was a bit short and left the ankles uncovered.

I have a sneaking suspicion that one of the legs of the pyjama was a bit shorter than the other. Whether it was done with a purpose, a style statement or because of the way he wore it was difficult to guess.

However, he paid a lot of attention to how others dressed. Once, I was busy taking an important staff meeting in my office when I received his call.

"Mr Mishra, why is your DIG wearing this funny cap?" The conversation started with this question.

I was totally flabbergasted and couldn't understand what he meant. I just managed to say, "Which DIG, Sir?"

"Your DIG is addressing the press wearing a golf cap. I don't care if he wants to cover his bald head. Tell him that he cannot wear such caps. Are you not watching him on the TV just now?"

By then, I had gathered my wits.

"Very unfortunate, Sir," I said. "He should not wear such caps. It is unbecoming of an officer."

My reply pleased him.

"Yes, very unbecoming. He should not appear in such caps. You should tell him firmly immediately."

"Yes, Sir."

The conversation ended. I had to dismiss my meeting and quickly found out which DIG had appeared before the press. I called him and told him not to be seen in that cap anymore.

A person should always be allowed to have his own personal space. The boss was very particular about this. Rarely did one see him getting physically close to people or even shaking hands with others. It is very common to see people in political life getting close to their supporters, patting them, holding their hands or even hugging them, but he hated all this.

Once, when he was still a minister at the centre, he visited the Raj Bhavan one evening to call on the governor. After his meeting, he was walking out when Mr Haridevan, the secretary to the governor, saw him from his room.

Mr Haridevan was a benign person but had a strong weakness for the stimulating sip. He was somehow convinced that if one had to consume any liquid, it should only be the elixir of life. Hence, one always found this gentleman, who had such noble thoughts, in a state of utter bliss and high spirits. That evening, when he found the great leader walking close to his office, the spirited Mr Haridevan rushed out and stood in front of him.

Being a benign and large-hearted person, he started the conversation by saying that a great leader like him should come back to the state. The people of the state and he, in particular, were waiting for him.

"Thank you very much," the great leader responded with a smile.

The large quantity of spirits in Mr Haridevan's system had loosened his inhibitions to a considerable extent. Thinking that the smile was a good invitation, Mr Haridevan hugged the leader and remained in that position for quite some time. It is difficult to say how the great leader finally managed to free himself before he rushed back to his car and fled.

Once, he came to Odisha on a visit. Among the many things that he had to take care of was Mr Haridevan. He called his secretary and asked him, "Golak *Babu*, where is that drunkard who had hugged me in the Raj Bhavan?"

"When was this, Sir?"

"Oh, I had come from Delhi to meet the governor and this secretary came from nowhere and hugged me. He was sozzled and reeking of cheap alcohol."

"I am really sorry, Sir."

"Don't be sorry. Just keep that bugger out of this place. He should not be seen anywhere near me."

"Ok, Sir."

That was how Mr Haridevan's career started or rather ended in the new regime.

Like many, I also firmly believed that running a government and administration was a very serious task. One had to look after so many things and make correct decisions on time. One was reminded of the subject, 'Evolution of the state', from our college days. I was particularly impressed by the theory of Thomas Hobbes, in which he stated that the state was essential to protect individuals from the dangers of the state of nature. Life in the state of nature, he professed with a lot of conviction, was solitary, nasty, brutish and short.

I had never discussed this with my professor, but I had a nagging feeling that this Hobbes must have gone through a harrowing experience at the hands of some dangerous felon or gang. Maybe someone had pulled his hair, scratched his face or made some horrendous sound in the proximity of his ear when he was possibly taking a short nap, thus putting him in a state of terrible fright. Else, I saw no reason why he would have used such strong adjectives and that too, four of them.

Anyway, whatever the reason, Hobbes seems to have been correct. Unless we have someone, who is strong-willed and decisive, to put an end to the acts of such desperados, life can be hell. This theory was absolutely relevant to our state, which was witnessing a kind of reversal of the state of nature in many parts due to the activities of the Naxalites. The need of the hour was a leader who was not only anti-brutish but also determined to put this nasty business to bed.

Often, meetings had to be held with the chief to apprise him of the developments and arouse in him an even stronger resolve to fight the brutes. In all his meetings, he would invariably have at least two of his advisors by his side. They formed the inner core and could pick up his highly codified signals like the Cheshire cat grin, the movement of his head, his smile or even his frown. I had to be part of many such meetings, especially the important ones to deal with the evolving Naxal situation.

"Sir, we have a situation developing on the border of Ganjam and Kandhamal. A large group has been sighted."

There was no reaction from him. He looked around and finally said, "The cook was at his best yesterday." He again looked around and grinned slightly. The advisors responded with broader grins. After some time, he gave me an enquiring look.

Not at all conversant with the signals of the court, I took it as one to continue.

"Sir, we have launched an operation involving our special groups and the district police."

"Oh! The taste of the minced meat still lingers."

There was another round of grins.

"Sir, we expect our commandos to reach the point by midnight."

"Don't you think the minced meat stuffed in the bekti fish was simply superb?"

"It was really good, Sir," one of the advisors confirmed.

I was feeling out of sorts and thought there was no point in taking the serious subject of fighting the Naxals any further. I decided to join the courtiers and grinned back.

"The taste of the fish mixed with the meat was delightfully superb. The cook is really turning out to be a fine culinary artist, a connoisseur."

Like Thomas Hobbes, he was freely using adjectives but for a totally different purpose.

The previous day, he had invited a person who had supposedly researched and written a lot on the subject of extremism. A luncheon meeting had been organised for him. This particular item, a fish stuffed with minced meat, was the dish of the day. We had been part of the luncheon group.

On another occasion, during a meeting, he desired some potato chips to be served. Promptly, one of the advisors ran out and ordered for them. This meeting was one in which our logistic build-up was being discussed.

"Sir, we are planning to move one of the CRPF battalions from Keonjhar district to Ganjam," I began.

At this point, the chips arrived and were served to us. He took out the paper napkin kept under the plate and closely examined it. It was pink.

"Mr Das," he roared at his principal advisor. "Do you think it is Valentine's Day?"

There was stunned silence.

"Pink napkins? Couldn't you find white ones?" He unfolded the napkin and started examining it more closely. "My God! It has little hearts printed on it."

There was a frown on his face.

Mr Das, who was squirming in his seat, suddenly got up and dashed out. He came back, followed by one of the servants, carrying white napkins. The offending pink napkins were replaced.

"Destroy them. I don't want to see them again," the chief commanded.

The meeting ended. Maybe, he was building up a proper anti-brutish personality with a fish and chips diet.

He was simply unable to take any decision without his advisors. Many times, it was necessary to meet him on a one-to-one basis. If a request was made, he would agree to it. He would listen to whatever I had to say, maybe ask a few questions and then say, "Mr Mishra, please write down all the points that we have discussed. I will get back to you."

I had to write them down and he would carefully keep the paper with him. His decision was conveyed only after he showed it to his trusted lieutenants. I wondered whether there was a necessity for a one-to-one meeting with him.

Meetings with visiting high-ranking officers from other states or the centre were conducted in a similar manner. After the initial pleasantries and listening to them, there used to be rarely any response from him. If the person persisted in talking, as many usually do, he would give a pitiful look as if to ask why we were not taking him away. This was a signal for the meeting to end.

Once he got a taste of power and found our race on the whole and the public representatives in particular to be really submissive, he developed a sense of disdain and a 'couldn't care less' attitude. He was never comfortable in the company of these people.

He soon started giving them nicknames, which were certainly uncharitable. There were two very senior ministers who had been members of the party for long. Their dark complexion prompted him to name them as 'niggers'. Similarly, a senior police officer, who again was dark and had managed to develop a rotund shape, was called 'black football' and so on and so forth.

The advisors, who either were or had come down to the same level of mental abilities as their boss, were entertained on hearing these nicknames, thereby fanning his perversions further. One often wondered if the whole scenario unfolding before us was real or a bad dream!

Will these bad days ever end? Sadly, the people of Odisha are yet to wake up.

# Doggy Tales

It was always a great joy listening to Mr Mishra narrating old events in his inimitable style. He had a photographic memory and could go into minute details as if the incident had happened only yesterday.

That day, we had gathered in his room at the police headquarters. Mr Mahapatra, the DIG (Signals), was also present. Mr Mishra started recounting his days as SP of Mayurbhanj district, where he had had to contend with the famous Mr Singh as his DIG.

The DIG had come for the inspection of the reserve office at Baripada. Mr Mishra reached the circuit house in the morning to accompany him to the parade ground where the inspection was to start with a ceremonial parade but found him in no state of preparedness. He was relaxing in his pyjamas and smoking.

"*Sala* orderly forgot to pack my shoes."

Mr Singh had taken upon himself the onerous task of preserving the British legacy of treating subordinates with disdain. He was convinced that they should be kept under a firm hand without any latitude for respect or mercy. How could he be less than any English officer? After all, he had been educated in London and had obtained a post-graduate degree in English. To be an effective British-type officer, one had to work on a strong vocabulary of abuses and profanities. He had worked on these quite meticulously.

"He didn't pack your shoes?"

"I have asked the blighter to come with the shoes on a bus. Of course, at his own cost," he added.

"Oh."

"He will reach around 2 pm. We will have the parade at 4."

"4 pm, Sir?"

"Yes."

It was a bit of an unusual time for a ceremonial parade, but who was to question the wisdom and English ways of Mr Singh?

He was ready at the appointed hour and accompanied the SP to the parade ground. On reaching the rostrum, his gaze was fixed on some distant place and he started waving his baton, shouting, "Hass! Hass!"

Seeing this, Mr Mishra was quite intrigued and enquired, "What is it, Sir?"

"*Sala kutta.*"

Mr Singh did not discriminate between men and animals while using cuss words. '*Sala*' was emerging as his favourite one.

There was a stray dog some two hundred metres away.

Mr Mishra said, "I don't know why he was so scared of that dog."

Mr Mahapatra interjected, "You don't know? He had a terrible experience involving a dog."

Many years ago, one Mr Joseph used to be the assistant inspector general. He was a no-nonsense type of officer, meticulous in his work and had the ear of the inspector general. Officers were of the firm opinion that one had to first impress Mr Joseph if one was to do well in the department.

One day, Mr Singh, who was in the early stages of his career, decided to call on Mr Joseph. As this was his first visit, he thought it would be appropriate to take two others along with him. Mr Mahapatra and another officer were chosen to accompany him. He was sure that with these two around, he would certainly be able to make a mark with his impeccable English.

The three of them reached Mr Joseph's house in the evening and marched up to the veranda. What they did not know was that Mr Joseph had a dog of good German pedigree, who had grown up to a formidable size. Unfortunately for these three, the dog, like his master, was also a firm follower of the no-nonsense school of thought. The moment he caught the scent of the visitors, he rushed out with a sharp bark.

Shaken to the core by this unanticipated danger, Mr Mahapatra and the other gentleman decided to flee. As they didn't have much time to reach the gate, they ran towards the boundary wall with the Alsatian in close pursuit. Somehow, they managed to jump over the wall and reach the road. The dog, well-trained as he was, decided to end his pursuit and displayed no intentions of chasing them once they had jumped out of the private property under his watch and turned back.

Mr Singh had spent much of his younger days in the pursuit of English literature and in imbibing the various traits of British officers. In the process, he had possibly neglected to develop the ability to break into a quick sprint at such short notice. Moreover, the sudden appearance of a huge dog had momentarily numbed his senses and as a result, he continued standing on the veranda, stupefied. On seeing Mr Singh, the dog started rushing towards him to continue his solemn duty of clearing the premises of unwanted intruders.

Not knowing what to do in such an exigency, Mr Singh thought he could put his command of English to good use. He did not have much time to deliver a moving speech but managed a few sharp English commands like Stop, Go and the like. On a pedigreed dog, well set on his mission, these words had no effect and there was no visible change in his mindset. Mr Singh decided to take evasive action by hiding behind various pieces of furniture placed on the veranda. The strategy adopted was not much of a success as the dog was unrelenting in his pursuit.

In his hurry to evade the charging dog, Mr Singh made a rather quick move that unbalanced him and he fell on the floor. For a moment, even the dog was startled, but after realising that he was in no danger from a man in the prone position, he decided to pounce on him. Instinctively, Mr Singh used his hands to ward off the dog, but, in the process, got bitten severely. To escape from further bites, he caught hold of a small teapoy and started waving it at the dog, shouting, "Hass! Hass!", hoping that the dog would be forced to run away. The desired result was not achieved; rather, this enraged the dog further, who went down to evade the teapoy and bit Mr Singh's leg.

Realising that the matter could not be handled by him any longer, Mr Singh cried out for help. Somebody came and found him in this pitiable condition. The dog and Mr Singh were separated with some effort. Whether he could meet Mr Joseph after all this was not very clear.

The incident left such a lasting impression on Mr Singh that he could no longer bear even the sight of a dog. His hatred for dogs was further reinforced when his son had to face a bad chase from another pet dog belonging to a junior officer.

It seems Mr Singh's son had gone to meet his friend, the son of Mr Verma. The Vermas were also dog lovers and had very lovingly kept a Spitz, a small-sized dog with a white coat. Their pet was raised as a member of the family and used to roam around freely in the house.

That day, on seeing junior Singh, the dog barked. Junior Singh was well aware of his father's traumatic experience. The bark was enough to start him off. He did not want to repeat his father's mistake and be anywhere around the dog.

Jr. Singh ran with good speed, but the dog decided to take up the challenge. Unfortunately, this dog was not very conversant with the concept of private and public property. Whereas Mr Joseph's Alsatian had rightly decided to end his chase at the boundary wall, this Spitz ran with all its might behind Jr. Singh even when he had cleared the private property and had hit the public road.

The chase continued up to Mr Singh's residence. On seeing the gate of his house, the boy let out a big shout for help as the dog seemed to be catching up with him. Someone opened the gate and let the boy inside. The gate was closed instantly, ending the pursuit of the determined dog.

Hearing the commotion, Mr Singh came out and found his son panting. Learning about the incident, he fumed with rage. At this stage, the Spitz, deprived of the opportunity to finish the race in a most unfair manner, gave a bark from the other side of the gate, startling Mr Singh to the core.

"*Sala kutta*!" he screamed and ran inside with his son.

***

Once, I had to face such a situation. My elder brother had come from Bhubaneswar and wanted me to accompany him to the house of the then DGP to invite him to my niece's marriage. We did not have the faintest clue that the DGP was also a dog lover and had a good number of Dachshunds, another species from Germany. No prior appointment was fixed since it was a holiday and we presumed the DGP would be at home.

Both of us reached his house in the early evening and entered the premises. As we were approaching the porch and the steps leading to the veranda, a person came out, followed by a pack of these Dachshunds. Their sudden appearance was certainly unnerving, but I had a feeling that the dogs were equally unnerved on seeing us. They started barking in unison, making a racket and rushed towards us.

My brother showed exceptional presence of mind and nimbleness. In a fraction of a second, he jumped and placed himself on a ledge, away from the marauding pack.

His acrobatics did not go down well with the dogs. That an intruder could come in and jump in front of them was a bit too much for them to take calmly. They decided to come near the ledge and climb up. Fortunately for my brother, their short legs were not enough to take them up to that position. Standing on two legs and doubling their efforts to climb up, they continued barking.

I was sure that I would meet the fate of Mr Singh or maybe much worse. Dachshunds can be quite aggressive and have a habit of coming from the rear and biting with ferocity. Here was a situation where they could surround me. I had decided that, if at all they started coming towards me, I would give the leader a good kick. After all, they were small and certainly more manageable than the one with which Mr Singh had to battle.

At this stage, another person came out to survey the scene. I chastised him for letting so many dogs roam around freely, posing grave danger. Somehow, he, along with that other person, could control the pack and take them inside. It was a close shave for both of us.

***

There used to be a commissioner of income tax in Bhubaneswar who also was a dog lover and had a big German Shepherd in his house. This dog, for some reason – either because of a bad upbringing or some mutation in his genes – had badly strayed from the rich traditions of Germany. He had somehow adapted to the Indian ways and had grown to be a great lover of food, with a particular liking for the food served to the guests who visited the commissioner. He was not much bothered about guarding the house but was very concerned that food from the house should not be consumed by outsiders. After all, why should food go to others when he was there?

Once the guest had settled down and it was time for snacks or some eatables to be served, the dog would catch the scent and arrive at the scene and keep a keen watch on the movement of the guest. The moment the guest made a move to touch the food, the dog would growl and come rushing towards him. His growl and movement were enough for any guest to go into a fear-induced trance. Thereafter, he would eat whatever was on the plate and depart.

Once, a friend of mine, a deputy commissioner in the department, had gone to visit the commissioner. Some sweets and snacks were served. The commissioner asked him to eat them quickly or else the dog would come and eat the snacks.

There was no dog in sight but not knowing what to do, the poor fellow picked up a sweet. In a flash, the dog, watching from somewhere, reached him, snatched the sweet from his hands and started eating it. The snatching process was so swift that the fingers of the deputy commissioner were badly bruised by the sharp incisors of the Indianized German dog. He sat transfixed in his chair, while the dog took his own time to gobble up everything on the plate and then left.

I had wanted to meet the commissioner, but after learning about the habits of this dog, thought it prudent to drop the idea.

***

The police department had introduced canine breeds to help in the detection of cases. Pups of good breed were chosen and trained to develop and fine-tune their olfactory senses to such an extent that they could follow the scent and connect the crime to the criminal. They were under the charge of trained handlers who not only took care of their food and grooming but also put them through rigorous training. These dogs would stop, run, sleep, salute and shake hands on command, much to the awe and admiration of people who had never seen dogs behaving in this manner.

These dogs and their handlers were made available to each district and were deployed for detection work whenever a big crime was reported. Sambalpur was a big district and because of the large number of cases, two dogs were available. Mr Mohanty, who was the SP of the district, was extremely thorough in his work and was a perfect example of an officer who always went by the book. He would never compromise on matters of discipline and for that, he wanted all the men under his charge to be put through physical training and parade on a regular basis.

The weekly ceremonial parade was held regularly and in a very proper way. All officers and men present at Sambalpur had to attend the parade. One day, Mr Mohanty realised that the two dogs and their handlers, who were very much part of the force under his command, were not attending this parade. Immediate orders were issued that the dogs and the handlers should remain present for the next parade. The reserve inspector was summoned along with the handlers and it was decided that the dogs would sit in front of the rostrum on both sides of the steps. Since the dogs were trained, the handlers were to remain behind the rostrum.

The dogs belonged to different breeds. While one was a German Shepherd, the other one was a relatively uncommon breed called the Dobermann. Though both had been subjected to the same training and discipline, they had different personality traits. While the German

Shepherd was calm and composed, the Dobermann had a muscular disposition and was known for its aggressive nature. However, both sat calmly by the side of the steps and were watching the proceedings with keen interest.

The SP arrived at the appointed time and climbed the dais. He received the salute from the parade and now it was time for the reserve inspector, who was commanding the parade, to march towards the rostrum, salute the SP with his sword and then invite him to inspect the parade. The inspector started marching smartly with his sword held upright and came towards the rostrum. He reached near the steps, halted, then lifted the sword up to his face and with a fine move, dipped it down for the final act of salute. The Dobermann, watching the proceedings with intent, was badly startled by this dipping of the sword in such proximity and thought it was a prelude to an attack. He sprang up from his sitting position and with a loud growl, rushed towards the inspector.

The German Shepherd did not want to be left behind on this important mission and decided to join in, growling and charging from the other side. The reserve inspector is one who is trained in strategic moves and manoeuvres, but this particular one was badly affected by the sudden charge from two good-sized dogs from two sides. He adapted to the emergency quite well, crouching down to a pose adopted by seasoned swordsmen and waving the sword with good speed, pointing it at the muzzle of the dogs. Continuing this procedure of keeping the dogs at bay, he started taking steps backwards to distance himself from the two.

The SP was also badly affected. Even though the dogs did not pose any direct challenge to him, it was beyond his comprehension that trained dogs could behave like this. He just could not bear the sight of this indiscipline and started shouting, "Handler! Handler!"

The handlers who were behind the rostrum had not anticipated that their wards would let them down so badly. The handler of the Dobermann thought it appropriate to vanish from the scene, but the other one took charge and with loud commands of "Stop! Stop!", somehow managed to halt the dogs. By then, the inspector had also covered substantial ground with his backward steps. The dogs were leashed and taken back to the kennel and the parade was completed.

The next day, both the handlers were seen undergoing a punishment drill.

***

Another interesting episode involving a police dog was reported from Mayurbhanj district and it happened on 26 January, when the Republic Day functions were being held. A senior minister from Bhubaneswar had been deputed to be the chief guest at the district parade. The SP had introduced an event where the police dog would display his skills in detection and this was to take place immediately after the march-past was over. Soon after the parade, the platoons had moved out and the entire ground was empty. The chief guest was seated on the dais and many people who had come for the parade were watching with keen interest as the dog and his handler appeared.

The dog gave a good display of his obedience and performed all the acts as per his handler's commands. The onlookers were absolutely thrilled. The handler then took the show to a different level when he started displaying the abilities of the dog in scent work. A handkerchief was obtained from someone standing near the fence and the dog was given the scent. Immediately, the dog ran towards the fence and started barking at the person who had given the handkerchief. The crowd roared in approval. The minister also looked very impressed.

The handler could not control his excitement. He took the dog to the dais and produced a pack of cards. The minister was requested to pick one card, hold it for some time and then mix it in the pack. The dog took the scent from the minister's shoes and started looking for the card in the pack. After a while, he got one and gave it to the handler. It was the card that the minister had picked. The minister was so impressed that he got up and handed a cash reward to the handler.

"How do you manage all this?" he wanted to know.

The handler was now fully charged up. "Sir," he started with a flourish, "I have trained him in everything. The dog does exactly what I say. He will eat, sleep, get up and do anything only at my command."

"Oh! Very good."

The handler had to leave with his dog as the minister had other programmes on the dais.

As the dog and the handler left the ground, they had to pass by the minister's car parked nearby. The dog, fresh from his scent work, picked up the smell of the tyres and like any dog, could not resist the temptation of lifting his leg and directing a strong jet at a tyre. The handler, realising that the minister's car was being vandalised, pulled the dog and in the process, the jet, which the trained dog had so nicely directed at the tyre, now fell on the door of the car and made a complete mess.

The driver, who was nearby, saw what had happened and howled in disapproval. The handler and the dog quickly left the scene, but the driver was convinced that it was a serious matter and had to be reported forthwith. He rushed to the minister and narrated the incident, adding that he had a suspicion that the whole act was intentional. The handler had already said that the dog did everything only at his command. Hence, this act of sacrilege must have been planned by the handler, too. The minister's team was convinced that it was part of a conspiracy to humiliate the minister. The matter was taken up strongly with the district magistrate and the SP and strong action was demanded against the handler. Somehow, with a lot of persuasion, the matter was resolved.

***

My personal experience with dogs and their moods goes back to the years when I was in college. My brother had a German Shepherd named Jolly, who was a part of our family. She was a good-sized dog and had built up a fair reputation for scaring people. Like most home dogs, she had not been exposed to any professional training. Whatever way she behaved was through self-learning.

In the process, she had developed habits, which she liked. She would resist being in chains, bark on seeing people, bare her teeth and threaten us if something was not to her liking and above all, took great pride in scaring unsuspecting people who walked into the house. She spent the most part of the day on our outer veranda, chained to the door, giving her a good view of the gate and would bark furiously on seeing anyone entering and jump up and down as if she would break loose.

There were particular times when she was unchained. She had built up a good relationship with my twin brother and me and on seeing us, would plead to be unchained and play with us. We never let her down. During those periods when she was free, it was time for her to play and wander around the house, but the moment she heard the sound of the gate, she would rush out and run to the visitor, barking.

Now, there were two types of visitors. There were some who had great reliance on their speed. On seeing the dog, they usually ran back and closed the gate. There were some who had either advanced too far inside the house or were unable to generate high speed for their retreat.

They were the ones who had to face very traumatic times. One could hear them scream, shout, jump and do many things, which they had never done before. Some were too numbed to even speak.

However, Jolly never crossed the line and did not cause any physical harm by way of biting any intruder. Her sole motto was to instil a sense of fear. After all, she had an assigned role in the family.

One evening, we heard some kind of cry followed by a yelp, which sounded like coming from a dog. Going out to investigate, we found Jolly rushing inside with her tail between her legs. On going further, a man was found lying near a bed of marigold flowers and crying. He was lifted up and brought to the veranda.

"Did she bite you?" asked my father, very concerned.

"Ooooooo...," he continued crying.

My brother was examining him minutely for any signs of injury. He asked the man, "Are you hurt?"

There was a stronger 'Oooooooo' in reply. The man was in a state of deep shock and in no condition to speak.

My father asked, "Where is Jolly?"

She was found hiding under a bed.

After a few glasses of water and constant cajoling, the man started getting back to normal and could speak but very feebly.

From what we could gather, he had come to meet my brother. However, he had no idea that the house had a dog. He opened the gate and as he was walking in, found the dog coming towards him. In that moment of panic, he ran towards a bed of marigold plants. The plants had grown rather tall, and he thought they would provide him good cover. For a dog familiar with the terrain, the marigold bed was no hindrance as she pursued the intruder with a strong determination and found him. The gentleman made a valiant effort in running around the bed with a good amount of vigour but had to reduce his speed considerably at the sharp bends and then again accelerate. This merry-go-round continued for a while.

"How did you fall?"

"I don't know. Perhaps I collided with the dog."

"Collided?"

"Yes."

From his ramblings, I could somehow gather that at some stage of the running around the bed, it was either the man or the dog who, for some reason, abruptly changed direction. As a result, there was a head-on collision between the two. The man fell on the dog. Jolly, who had never experienced such a heavy weight falling on her and that too after a collision, got frightened to such an extent that she gave a yelp and ran inside for safety.

The man, already in a state of panic and running desperately to evade the charging dog, was stunned by the collision and consequent fall. In the darkness, he could not see properly what had happened and was not even sure that the dog had left the scene. In that helpless condition of not being able to move and see, he possibly thought that he was at the mercy of the dog. That fear in his mind about the dog took a long time to subside.

He was again becoming very emotional recalling the turn of events. The moment he felt he could manage to walk, he left our house.

My father decided to put a board on the gate saying, BEWARE OF THE DOG. He did not want a repetition of the events.

***

I had never thought of keeping a pet in the house after joining the service. Much later, when my daughter and son were growing up, they kept insisting on having a dog at home. I had asked a few people I knew to find out if a good pup was available.

One day, a close associate informed me that he had a German Shepherd pup and asked if I would be interested in having it. The children were ecstatic with the offer and the pup, which was about three months old.

It had the features of a German Shepherd, but if one looked carefully at his face, one could detect strong hints of a mix with a terrier or some other breed. He had a lot of facial hair, more in the eyebrows and around the muzzle and a good amount of fluff under the chin. He looked very cute to us with his beard and the children aptly named him Prince, but to someone who saw him for the first time, his looks were quite disturbing, like those of a ferocious hound.

Prince grew up well in the company of my son and daughter. He was always allowed to move around freely in the house as the children were very particular about his personal liberty. He was quite friendly with people visiting us, but a few were so terrified by his looks that they used to shriek on seeing him and some even preferred to run away. One thing we noticed was that he never barked. As he grew to his full size by the tenth month, his failure to bark was an issue that needed attention. I decided to get professional help. A trainer was contacted, and he came to see Prince.

"What is the problem?" he wanted to know.

"He doesn't bark," my wife said.

"Doesn't bark?"

"No."

The trainer looked quite perplexed. It was something quite new to him and was possibly beyond his curriculum. He thought for some time and then said, "I will come tomorrow."

The next day, he arrived, carrying a gunny bag with him.

"What is this bag for?" we asked.

"Sir, wait. Where is the dog?"

The dog was summoned. The trainer looked at him intently and then called us aside. He said, "I will enter from the gate. You can keep the dog here so that he has a clear view."

He disappeared. After some time, we found him near the gate with the gunny bag covering him. Immediately, he went down on all fours and started crawling.

I was quite taken aback by his methods. There was a serious doubt in my mind whether this trainer could actually train or needed to be trained. As these doubts were crossing my mind, the trainer had covered quite a distance with his crawl and was coming closer towards us. I found Prince, who was silent all along, looking at the crawling man quite intently. He let out a sound that sounded like a growl and before we could even realise what was happening, he rushed out barking furiously and reached the trainer.

All of this happened so suddenly that the trainer did not even have time to get up from that crawling position. Prince jumped on him and we had to resort to a lot of force to get him away from the trainer. The man stood up, quite shaken, but had a look of satisfaction on his face. After all, he had made the dog bark.

"Why did you put on that gunny bag?" I wanted to know.

He just smiled in reply. It was a secret he did not want to reveal. Perhaps, he wanted to look like a bigger dog to create a sense of fear in the non-barking dog. Anyway, the dog started barking, much to our relief. With his looks and his newly acquired ability to bark, Prince became quite a formidable force. His reputation as a dangerous dog spread all around and anyone coming to our house had to think twice before doing so.

***

I was posted to Kolkata, and we had to shift residence. I was allotted a big flat in the Garden Reach area on the first floor. The flat had a lovely veranda overlooking the garden and the road.

One day, a tailor came to our house to take my measurements for stitching a shirt. We were standing on the veranda while he went about his work. I was facing the garden. He had measured my chest, shoulders and arms and had put the tape around my neck to measure it. This should not have taken much time, but I found that the tailor kept on holding the tape around my neck.

I could hear his breathing become gradually heavier and the tape around my neck started tightening. It was a matter of concern for me. I looked at him and found that his gaze was fixed somewhere away from my neck and the tape. He was looking inside our living room and breathing rapidly. I followed his gaze and saw Prince casually walking towards us. As he came nearer, the tailor released the tape, rushed towards the edge of the veranda and tried to jump down. I asked him to stop and also shouted, "Prince! Go!"

Luckily, Prince obeyed my command, turned around and went inside.

The tailor was watching the proceedings wide-eyed, while still in a state of preparedness to jump. On seeing the dog turn around and go back inside the house, he relaxed a little but gave me a dirty look and asked, "You have kept him at home?"

I realised that on seeing Prince, the tailor had been under the impression that some wild animal had entered the house. He could not believe that such a fearsome animal could be kept at home. I assured him that Prince was a decent being and would not harm him. He did not seem convinced at all.

Before leaving, he wanted to clear his doubt. He asked, "Is it a dog?" I kept quiet, and he left.

***

Years later, we had a Labrador named Pluto. He was a real delight and a perfect home dog. Like all Labradors, he was extremely fond of company and would be very happy to have anyone in the house as long as he or she paid attention to him. Pluto travelled with us to Delhi when I went on transfer and adjusted well in the small flat. I used to take him out for his morning walks and he would be extremely happy. There are many pet dogs in the colonies in Delhi and on his walk, Pluto would see and cross many other dogs, either in the company of their masters or caretakers.

This fascinated him. He would strain at the leash, pulling away to have a good look at the passing dogs or rather an opportunity to sniff them. Of the many that he encountered, I could see that he was developing a particular liking for a small Dachshund, who came out in the company of her master. Shahjahan Road, the locality where we lived, housed very important people like ministers, secretaries, members of parliament and the like. The Dachshund and her master used to take a regular route every morning, and we used to cross each other.

The master, belonging to a higher echelon of the bureaucracy, had a stiff upper lip and displayed no emotion or signs of cheer or happiness even during those beautiful morning hours. For him, it was a compulsive routine that had to be followed and he did so with a grumpy face.

One morning, Pluto and I were a little late and hence, the grumpy master and the not-so-grumpy dog had moved some distance away. Pluto was in the mood to at least have a close look at his favourite.

He started straining at the leash and exerted such pressure that he was able to release the collar around his neck along with the leash. I was left holding the leash and collar and Pluto merrily rushed off towards the Dachshund. The situation became very tense as I saw Pluto reach the two.

What followed thereafter was quite a scene. On seeing Pluto coming near, the small dog, hitherto walking sedately by her master's side, ran towards his legs and clung to them. The master, on seeing the situation and Pluto close by, screamed, "Aaaieeee!"

Pluto, not accustomed to such a sound, ran back. Seeing him go away, the small dog came back to her normal position. Pluto took it as a signal to march forward, sending the small dog to cling to her master again, followed by another 'Aaaieeeee'.

This cycle continued for maybe four or five rounds before I thought I should intervene. I ran to the spot and on seeing me, the grumpy man gave me a look, which was far from friendly. "What is this?" he asked, pointing at Pluto.

He probably wanted to know why such a huge dog had been allowed to move around without a leash. I showed him the collar and leash. No further words were exchanged. A man of his stature did not feel it appropriate to engage in further conversation with me. I caught hold of Pluto, tightened the collar on his neck and dragged him away. For a week or so, I avoided the route of the grumpy man.

***

Man's best friend can be a source of great joy. Dogs somehow fill your life and make you a part of theirs. There can be many memorable moments that one recollects at leisure and relives the great times with those lovely companions.

However, stray dogs, who are found in plenty in any city or town, are often the source of serious traumatic experiences for many. Mostly, they are benign, but once in a while, you could encounter the dangerous types who stand in packs and suddenly decide to chase a passing car. As long as the driver and passengers are inside the car, they are safe from the dogs running behind it, but some of them start chasing people on two-wheelers. Once the chase starts, the poor riders become more concerned with protecting their legs from the charging pack than the traffic and keep looking back. As a result, they drive and that too fast, into unknown territories. Many have fallen into drains and some have dashed into oncoming traffic while evading these dogs.

I have spent many anxious moments, challenged by such dogs, while cycling. There was a pack of well-fed, good-sized street dogs inside Golf Links, a colony in Delhi. I used to cycle to the tennis courts and they would be sitting in the middle of the road that I took to reach my destination. My heart would sink at their sight. I had to take a half-kilometre detour just to avoid them.

This continued till I had to go to Japan for a training programme. The welcome kit contained a small book, which had instructions about the ways in Japan and in it, I finally found a solution to my problem.

One instruction was on how to avoid dogs. It was simple. All you had to do was avoid eye contact with a dog and ignore his presence. On my return, when I resumed my cycling, I reached the point in Golf Links where the street dogs were sitting. It was time to test the effectiveness of the procedure suggested. I started cycling towards them, looking the other way. Soon, I passed the pack. There was no response from them. The Japanese instruction was spot-on.

A week later, Tanaka, our Japanese friend in the tennis club, arrived with a bandage on his left calf.

"What happened?"

"I was bitten by a dog."

"How?"

"I was walking to the courts when one of the dogs suddenly charged at me and bit my leg."

"Did you look at his eyes?" I wanted to know.

"Of course, I looked at him when I was passing him."

What could I say? I told him about the useful instruction that I had learnt from a book about his country.

"Is it so? I did not know about this."

We have no dogs at home now, but I make it a point to follow the Japanese instruction whenever I see one.

Please try it. It works. Japanese techniques never fail.

## Outdoors

*When I feel like exercising, I just lie down until the feeling goes away.*

I had read somewhere some great man being quoted as saying this and started following this great piece of advice rather meticulously. After all, why should one make a conscious effort to cause pain to the body? I strongly believe that one should do only what pleases one.

I derived pleasure in playing games or going on a leisurely bike ride with friends. No one had to push me to undertake these activities. However, if I was asked to walk, run or even pump iron, it made no sense to me. After all, I could walk, run, play and cycle whenever I felt like it, so why this extra effort? Despite the best efforts of my father and other senior members of the family, I always strictly refused to get up early and undertake these pointless activities.

Once, while in college, a friend and I had been badly bitten by the bug of developing good biceps. In those days, gymnasiums were not in vogue. A classmate of ours had told us about some kind of arrangement he had made at home, which was being used by many to develop their muscles.

Both of us were greatly excited on hearing about this and immediately made up our minds to have a go at it. We strongly believed that a few visits should be enough to develop a well-sculpted body, like a Greek god. It was also decided that the best time to visit would be early in the morning as the best results were achieved around sunrise.

The early risers in the family were quite amazed to see me waking up and getting ready to leave at that hour and made some comments that were not too much to my liking, but I left, undeterred. My friend was ready and soon, both of us were on our way.

We had expected to find the place alive with activity, but when we reached it, we found the door locked. After quite a bit of knocking and a long wait, some sound was heard from inside. Our friend, bleary-eyed, dishevelled and dressed in some sort of underpants, appeared at the door and looked at us in disbelief. We reminded him of his promise to help tone up our muscles.

Reluctantly, he admitted us into the room and showed us some bricks. First, we were supposed to do push-ups, using those bricks for a stand.

"You start the push-ups and I will get ready and come."

Having said this, he disappeared. We thought that without guidance, even push-ups could be dangerous. We waited and waited, but he had possibly gone back to sleep. That the trainer would let us down so badly was something we had not anticipated. Looking around the room, we found a pair of dumbbells, a rickety bench, a rod and some disc-like weights.

Not knowing what to do with them, we decided to leave. Our goal of developing our biceps was forgotten. We cursed ourselves for having deviated from the golden rule of taking things easy. There wasn't anything wrong with our biceps, we convinced ourselves.

***

Things changed drastically after I joined the police. From a laid-back life, one landed in a situation, which brought about a sudden transformation. Waking up at unearthly hours of the morning became part of the routine. As if that was not enough, one was forced to do many things, which one had never imagined.

Things like rope climbing, front rolls, back rolls, pull-ups, jumping over a wooden horse and many more activities, which we had seen only in a circus, became a part of our curriculum. Fortunately, there were no lions, tigers or elephants to be dealt with. All this started affecting our bodies in a startling manner.

One felt fitter and lighter, had sound sleep and developed a zest for life. This continued for as long as we were under training. Once the training was over and we were back for our postings, life came back to normal again. The overwhelming urge to take things easy and lie down when one felt like exercising took over with a strong vengeance.

There was a short period of three months when we were sent to the state police training college. Life here was totally different from the well-structured routine in Hyderabad. The outdoor classes were much lighter, but some new varieties of circus acts had been put in place.

One such act was to go from one big tree to another at a distance of some thirty metres. Two ropes were tied from one tree to the other, running parallel to each other. One had to climb up the tree, catch hold of both the ropes and then lie, facing down. Both the legs were placed on the two ropes. The body was held in place only by the hands and legs. Then one had to stretch the arms forward and pull so that the entire body slid forward.

By stretching, pulling and sliding, one had to reach the other tree. As if this in itself was not enough, we were asked to carry a rucksack and rifle on the back.

I was chosen as the first one to perform this acrobatic activity. I climbed up, held the rope and lay down. Then I stretched my arms and pulled.

"Very good." There was loud applause from below.

Encouraged, I stretched again. The moment I started to pull, the rope on my right sagged. As a result, I turned sideways and instead of looking at the ground, started looking to the left. In this position, the rucksack and rifle on my back also moved sideways. I clung to the ropes desperately.

I could hear the trainers making all kinds of alarmed sounds like, 'Ohooo', 'Arreee'.

One of them asked the other, "Didn't you tie the ropes properly?"

The conversation and sounds did not do a bit of good to my sagging spirits. I was dangling precariously. My own weight, combined with that of the rucksack and rifle, was pulling me down. I could not last long and fell. Fortunately, I was recovered in one piece with no damage. The circus was closed for the day after this mishap.

***

While undergoing this training, we received intimation that we were to go to Cuttack to attend the senior police officers' conference. This conference was an annual event where all officers met for two days and discussed professional matters. As greenhorns, it would be our first exposure to this group of elites.

Off we went to Cuttack and reached on time. We were accommodated in Bhubaneswar along with some others. These included one Mr Sandhu, who was senior to us by one year but behaved as if he had fifteen years of experience. The second day, when we were having breakfast, we learnt that after the conference, we were all supposed to attend the closing function of the annual sports day of the police.

It had also come to our notice that the function included a hundred metres run for officers. Just to keep abreast with facts, I thought of asking

Sandhu about the race and whether we should carry our running dress, like shorts and T-shirts.

"What? Don't be silly," he exploded.

I could not make out what was silly about this normal query.

He clarified, "You are supposed to run in whatever you are wearing. Nobody goes with shorts and running shoes."

"Oh."

"Yes. Just join the race in your normal clothes."

We attended the conference and afterwards, went to the ground. The police sports day was a grand spectacle. The DG, other senior officers and many retired IGs had assembled for it. The last event for the evening was announced, the much-awaited gazetted officers' race. We took off our jackets and ties and proceeded towards the starting line.

On the way, I saw an officer changing his shoes and putting on proper running shoes with spikes. "Sandhu hadn't told us the full truth," I thought. We reached the starting line and were waiting when I saw someone joining the line from the side. On closer examination, I found it was Sandhu.

He was dressed in shorts, a T-shirt and white shoes. I looked at him in disbelief, but he avoided any eye contact with me. He had told us to wear normal clothes. Anyway, the line was put to order and the command for the start of the race followed. On the firing of the gun, everyone rushed off. I could see the officer with spikes shooting off in great style.

He was closely followed by Sandhu. Around the 50-metre mark, as I was closing in on Sandhu, a terrible incident happened.

There were many ladies in the cheering crowd and Sandhu, on seeing them, possibly had a heavy dose of adrenaline released in his system. As an effect, he started running at a higher speed. After all, he wanted to prove to the ladies that he was no less than Milkha Singh. His sudden acceleration unsettled him quite badly and I found Sandhu spreading his arms sideways and trying to regain his balance. Unfortunately, at that speed, he could not steady himself and fell on the tracks, blocking my way. I had to stop.

Onlookers from the side rushed in and lifted Sandhu. One retired IG, who had headed the force years ago, came up to Sandhu, looked at him with some concern and asked, "Gentleman, what is your problem? You had a similar fall last year as well. Is everything okay with you?"

I did not hear Sandhu's reply but learnt something about this perfidious character. That was our initiation to the famous GOs' race.

A few years later, when I was posted as AIG, we had again lined up at the starting point for the race. Sandhu was nowhere to be seen. He had abandoned the idea of the race after two successive falls. A sizeable crowd gathered near the starting line to watch the senior officers run. We were all ready, waiting for the call and the gunshot. I had positioned myself at the extreme end on one side.

It was all quiet and the starter call was expected when I heard some kind of hissing sound coming from near my right knee. Startled, I looked down and was quite shocked to see Mr Fidgety in a position, which accomplished sprinters like Jesse Owens and the like take. His hands were on the line and his legs were stretched back.

For him, this was quite an effort, and it made him breathe fast and produce a sound like steam escaping at high pressure from some leaking pipe. He had somehow managed to squeeze himself into that position, very close to the crowd.

"Good evening, Sir," I greeted him. He was too focused on the race to even acknowledge my greeting. "Sir, why don't you stand upright like all of us? It will be easy to look ahead and stay clear of the crowd."

My helpful advice probably caused some kind of deep turmoil in his mind, making him breathe harder. Perhaps he was not taking my advice in the right spirit. Instead of irritating him further, I preferred to keep quiet and waited for the starter gun.

It went off, and the race started. Mr Spikes breezed past all and like every year, touched the finishing line with perfection. I did not see Mr Fidgety anywhere around the finishing line. Concerned, I made enquiries and found out that Mr Fidgety, on hearing the gunshot, had accomplished, with great finesse, the delicate task of springing up from that starting position but, because of some minor malfunctioning of the core muscles on his back, could not attain the firm upright position.

As a result, he had started running in a bent position for about ten metres. Before he could straighten up and look straight towards the finishing line, he had to abandon the race, as he had mistakenly proceeded sideways towards the crowd and got terribly mixed up with the spectators. However, he did run in style for about ten metres and the crowd of spectators received him in their midst with a lot of cheer.

The very next year, it was felt that the hundred-metre dash was proving to be too short an affair. Moreover, the fall of Sandhu and the disappearance of Mr Fidgety into the crowd raised issues of safety. Sudden sprinting, especially for people who had stopped doing even brisk walking, could be perilous.

The crowd was also being deprived of the enjoyment of watching this spectacle as the race was over in no time. It was decided that instead of a hundred metres, the race would now be 400 metres. It would go on for a longer time and meant that the great runners would have to take a full round of the ground.

The race was scheduled as the last event and the runners had lined up at the starting line. This time, there were not many participants as the prospect of running a full round was too much for most. Mr Spikes was ready and so were the others. However, the 400-metre dash proved to be a disaster of great magnitude.

Mr Spikes, an expert sprinter, started with the same speed with which he usually started the shorter race. He was way ahead of the others, but as he was approaching the 200-metre mark, one could see him wavering from one track to the other. He was not able to hold himself steady. Gasping badly for air, he realised that he would not be able to go any further and quietly ran inside a tent by the side of the tracks.

The others following him were moving at a slower pace. At this stage, I decided that it was time to pick up speed. As I accelerated, another officer, possibly with the same idea, also broke from the pack and came in my path. His legs got entangled with mine and he had a terrible fall.

He gave me a very scornful look, which, I felt, conveyed his feelings that I had intentionally tripped him. I had no heart to leave him lying like that, feeling that way. Looking at him with grave concern, I decided to help him up. By the time he was examined and found fit enough to restart, the race was over.

***

Odisha Police had another interesting activity, which required the participation of senior officers. It was the annual shooting competition. In those days, when we were new to the service, this was one event which generated a lot of enthusiasm. All districts and battalions sent their teams for this event and competed with each other for the laurels. It was compulsory for each team to have a senior officer of the rank of superintendent of police or a commandant.

Teams were chosen with great care and put into rigorous practice. The competition used to be held in the town of Dhenkanal, which had a very well-maintained shooting range. All the teams were put up in tents and the whole area looked like a lovely camping site. Along with the trophies for the best teams in rifle and revolver firing, this event, over the years, had developed a tradition of honouring the worst performing teams in both groups by presenting them with a wooden spoon.

To add insult to injury, the moment the team leader received the spoon, he had to stand in front of the crowd, holding it, while the band played a melancholic tune. In the evening, after the day's proceedings were over, every team would be busy calculating its scores, some to evaluate their prospects to get to the top and some to see whether they were closing in on the spoons.

One year, when I was representing Koraput district as the additional superintendent of police, I experienced the kind of atmosphere prevalent in the camp and during the shooting events.

Mr Das, posted in a battalion, was a very seasoned shooter and despite his seniority, he always insisted on taking part in the competition. He was a tall and well-built man, known for his rather mercurial and erratic behaviour. His aim was to win the trophy for the best officer in revolver shooting. He had been competing for it every year but could never succeed. Nonetheless, this had no effect on his great ambition and he would come back the next year with a lot of determination. His detail had fired for one of the events in the revolver competition. Each shooter had fired twelve shots. After the firing stopped, all the shooters marched to their targets to see the result.

The official scorer came before each target and recorded the hits and points scored. Mr Das was standing calmly when the scorer came and counted the hits. He could find ten holes. He looked hesitantly at Mr Das and said, "Sir, only ten hits. Two shots are washouts."

"Are you blind?" Mr Das exploded.

The scorer preferred to keep quiet. Mr Das rushed near the target and pointed at two holes.

"Can't you see? Two bullets have gone through these two holes. All twelve hits."

The scorer was not convinced. He called his superior. Both looked closely at the target and then at Mr Das. If they had any intention of discussing the matter with him, they decided to keep it on hold. From the looks of Mr Das and the way he was looking at them, they could anticipate that there was a great risk of physical assault if they raised the matter of the two washouts before him again. Using their discretion, they decided to somehow escape.

"Sir," they addressed Mr Das. "We are going to the tournament referee, Mr Mohammad, to settle this matter."

"Go anywhere you like." Saying this, Mr Das stood guard before his target as the two proceeded to the referee.

The referee, Mr Mohammad, was another character. He was the DIG of armed police and had been asked to oversee the competition and act as the referee and to adjudicate any dispute. He had the least interest in firing and took this work more as a punishment.

Both the scorers reached him and narrated the sequence of events and the insistence of Mr Das that two of his bullets had passed through the same hole.

"What? He can fire two bullets through the same place?"

"That is what he claims, Sir."

"Who is he to decide? We will go by what you have observed."

At this stage, someone behind Mr Mohammed prompted, "Sir, Mr Das is coming."

"Das? Where?"

Mr Das, standing guard near his target, realised that his presence during the arbitration would be of paramount importance. So, he decided to uproot his target and marched towards Mr Mohammad, carrying the target with him as conclusive evidence. After all, he had to show the referee the two disputed holes.

Before Mr Mohammad could look up, Das banged the target on his desk and stood before him.

"See," he thundered.

Mr Mohammad sprang up from his seat and looked pulverised.

"Oh, Das! Ha ha!" He flashed a sheepish grin.

Das was in no mood to exchange grins and gave the referee a stern look.

Mr Mohammed said, "I was just telling them. How can you miss hitting the target?"

Das continued to look at him sternly.

"I have awarded you all twelve hits. He he!" He grinned again.

Das picked up the target from the desk and marched away. He was in no mood to grin or discuss anything. All he meant was business.

Mr Mohammad gulped down a glass of water and murmured to himself, "Shouldn't this fellow be banned from next year?"

While Das got his points, Mr Lenka, the SP of Kalahandi district, was going through a bit of a bad patch. He had fared rather miserably in the rifle competition. Despite his strong background of having undergone guerrilla training, he had somehow not been able to keep his aim steady from the 300-metre mark.

Most of his bullets could not reach the target and hit the ground, raising clouds of dust. Having confirmed his team's last position in the rifle competition, he had now the responsibility of avoiding the same plight in revolver shooting. Determined to put up a good show, he lined up for the last item in revolver shooting.

This event required the competitors to stand at the 75-metre mark and then run to the 50-metre mark, lie down, load the revolver with bullets carried with them and fire. All this had to be done in one minute. For convenience, most of the firers held the bullets in one hand and then ran.

It was easy to load the revolver if one had the bullets in one's hand. For some reason, Mr Lenka decided to put the bullets in his trouser pocket. He ran the twenty-five metres at good speed, reached his position at the 50-metre mark and took the prone position. He then put his hand inside his pocket and searched for the bullets.

As he was lying down, his hand could not go all the way inside his pocket. He turned to his side and retrieved the bullets. By the time he was able to put only two bullets in the chamber, the shrill sound of the whistle shook him up. He looked up and found all the others getting up. The one-minute time was over.

Not knowing what to do, he stood up with his revolver and looked back at the inspector conducting the event and, in the process, pointed his revolver towards him. The inspector, on seeing the muzzle of a loaded revolver pointed towards him, was horrified and commanded him rather loudly to turn and face the target and unload his revolver. Mr Lenka turned around, fuming.

Not being able to fire a single shot, Mr Lenka ensured that his team safely qualified to earn the wooden spoon in revolver shooting as well. At the closing ceremony, he held the two wooden spoons with great humility. He did not seem much concerned about his performance but was certainly worried about the falling standards of discipline and decorum. Two issues rankled his mind. How could an inspector command him so sternly and why did they play a melancholic tune when he received the spoons?

Most of the districts and battalions that took the shooting competition seriously started their practice at least two months before the appointed date. While I was posted as SP in Rourkela, we started our practice for the competition in earnest along with the shooters and the commandant of a battalion located there. Our practice sessions were in the morning and used to go on for at least three hours.

One day, the DIG, Mr Fidgety, called me and enquired, "How is it that you are always in the firing range in the morning hours?"

"Sir, we are practising for the competition."

"So much practice is required?"

I kept quiet.

"Okay, I will come to the range tomorrow and maybe give you some tips."

He arrived the next morning when we were engaged in rifle firing from the 300-metre mark. He took the position, aligning himself to a target. He held the rifle, closed one eye and set his sights.

"Where is the target?"

"Can't you see it?"

"No."

"No?"

"What is all this? Why should you waste time firing from such a long distance? After all, in police work, you should be prepared for close-quarter battles. Where is the revolver range?"

We stopped the rifle shooting practice and took him to the revolver range. On seeing it, he gave a broad smile.

"Yes. This is perfect. I will now teach you a thing or two."

"Sir."

"Which procedure do you all follow when firing the revolver?"

"Procedure?"

"Don't you know? There are two types of procedures. One is the German method and the other, American."

"Oh."

"Let me show you the German method."

He held the loaded revolver and stood in front of the target. Instead of aiming the revolver straight at the target, he pointed it to the ground near his feet. We were watching intently.

"The Germans start from here and gradually lift the revolver in an arch and then fire the moment they align with the target," he advised.

He started lifting his hands gradually while pressing the trigger. Before his revolver could come to the level of the target, it went off with a loud bang and the bullet went to the ground. He jumped up, badly startled. However, to cover up, he lifted the revolver and fired at the target but missed it completely. He fired another shot, which again missed and went to the other side. He looked at me with a nervous grin.

"I am slightly out of practice. Shall we try the American method?"

"What is the American method, Sir?"

"It is the opposite. You get the revolver from above your head down towards the target."

I was worried that this man could cause a serious accident with his untested methods.

"Sir, shall we proceed to the tent? Your tea is getting cold."

He also seemed to be happy with this suggestion. He never came to the range again.

Institutionally, the annual shooting competition and the gazetted officers' race were the two outdoor activities in place where the involvement of officers was required. As years passed, one realised that these two activities were not enough to take care of one's physical well-being. It was entirely up to the concerned person to decide whether to exercise or become fat and rotund.

Many chose the path of least trouble and were not a bit shy in displaying pleasingly plump bellies, developed by years of good nourishment and complete abstinence from exercise. After about seven years of enjoying a similar life, I was quite alarmed one day when I stood before a mirror and realised that my belly was also showing definite signs of starting its journey to join the levels of rotundness displayed by others.

Shell-shocked, I made a strong resolve to put an end to it. Starting to exercise after such a long gap was an issue. An expert was called for advice. He suggested a series of exercises. I started with them in his presence, but the moment I was left to do them alone, it became such a boring and painful affair that I gave up.

A friend of mine had been accompanying me for morning walks, which we both had started just a few days before the arrival of the expert. One day, he saw me jumping, bending and doing all kinds of things, which he had never seen me do before. He watched both me and the expert keenly and when we started on our walk, he asked me, "Are you seriously thinking of doing those kinds of things daily?"

"It is quite difficult and boring," I agreed.

"You will never be able to go on with that kind of hard work."

"Why?"

"Have you heard the song, 'Love me little, love me long'?"

"No."

He was a well-read man and repeated the relevant portion of the song:

*Love me little, love me long,*

*Is the burden of my song.*
*Love that is too hot and strong,*
*Burneth soon to waste.*

Having judged me as an impetuous and bull-headed person, he wanted to put some sense into me.

"Do something that you can continue doing for a long time. Don't fall for these quick methods, which you will never be able to pursue beyond a point."

I pondered over his great wisdom and the lovely poem for some time and realised that they had a lot of merit.

The services of the expert were discontinued with immediate effect and my friend and I marched off on a joyous walk every morning. Whether it had any immediate effect on the waistline or not was a matter of debate, but at least, one had now started getting up early and also using the legs to good effect.

My transfer to Cuttack separated me from my friend and in the new station, I had to go for my walks alone. It was then that I decided to add a bit of running to my exercise routine, along with my walk. Soon, the phases of running increased, and I was, much to my own surprise, able to run for longer spells. That the simple act of running could throw up various issues of concern, I started to learn gradually.

In the eighties, physical activity by people in general had not really caught on. There were quite a few who had taken to walking, but the majority felt that the best way to spend the morning was either to sleep or have a good cup of tea at the street corner and engage in conversation with friends.

Running on the roads as an exercise was possibly unheard of. Running and sports were basically confined to grounds designated for the purpose. When I started running, the first thing I encountered was the looks of concern and sometimes, disbelief, on the faces of people whom I crossed.

Some felt that I was probably trying to escape from a scene of crime. They would look back to see if I was being chased by somebody or a policeman. Some would look concerned, feeling that I had most likely lost my mind. The most embarrassing moments were when some people would start clapping and shouting, "Faster, faster," as you crossed them.

One day, as I ran past a group of people gossiping at a tea stall, one of them saw me and stood up.

He came close to the road and shouted, "Close your mouth. Breathe through your nose."

What do you do with such people? I just ran past, waving at him, but he kept shouting, "Nose, nose."

The other issue, which was quite a matter of concern, was the great interest that the street dogs showed when they saw me running. They were used to people walking and cycling but were possibly new to seeing someone running. I had anxious moments on one or two occasions when a pack of these street dogs charged at me when I passed them.

In a state of severe fright, I let out a yell and stood still. This probably saved me as accelerating and trying to run away from them was fraught with serious danger. As I stopped, the people around started making all kinds of noises. Whether they were meant for the dogs or for me, I did not care to explore. All I can say is that I barely escaped. It was at this stage that I decided to have a few others join me during my run.

As if dogs were not enough, even the bovine species, known for their calm and composed behaviour, threw in some very challenging moments for me.

Once, while running, we took a turn into another lane and saw something that stopped us in our tracks. Two huge bulls had occupied the road, locking their horns in a fight. There were some people on either side, watching the proceedings with great interest. There was no way we could take that road. We had to turn around and run back to take another route.

On another occasion, as we entered a narrow lane, we saw a cow being fed by somebody, possibly the owner. The cow was enjoying the calm and quiet morning and the loving attention of her master when we entered the lane. Our steps in unison made quite a noise and startled the cow to such an extent that she lifted her tail and took off in a kind of gallop. The master was thoroughly baffled on seeing his gentle cow suddenly behaving like a wild horse.

He looked at us, convinced that we were responsible for it. Abusing us, he also ran behind to take control of the cow, who had, by now, established a good lead. Fortunately for us, the cow decided to take a sharp right turn into a by-lane and we ran away from the abusing master.

To avoid all this, I decided to go to a ground, which was used by many people on their morning walk. There was a walking track all around the ground. I started my run on the track and was happy that I was away from the nuisances that I faced on the road but soon realised that even the track had its own problems.

Morning walks, I found, were a great opportunity for socialisation and gossip. People had their own groups and would walk together, talking and laughing. In the process, they would cover the entire track, leaving no space for a runner to overtake them.

One day, as I was overtaking a group of ladies, one of them suddenly moved from the middle to the right side and straight into my path. I almost crashed into her but made a perilous sideward jump off the track into the bushes and then got back onto the track, saving myself from a very awkward situation, trying to explain that I had not caused this crash intentionally.

By this time, I was hooked on running and physical exercise to a great extent. For the purpose of cross-training, cycling, at least once a week, was introduced into my exercise regime.

While all this was going on in full swing, I got transferred to Delhi.

A new environment meant new adjustments in my routine.

I started with walking and running. Delhi had lovely public gardens like the Lodhi Gardens and Nehru Park, which were thronged by many walkers and runners. Unlike Cuttack, running was quite popular here and one could find many people of all ages running at different speeds. I used to enjoy my runs at the Lodhi Gardens and sometimes, for a change, at Nehru Park.

Unlike the peculiar situations I encountered in Cuttack, I found a new kind of menace in Delhi. I would see one person running at his pace ahead of me and the moment I reached near him to overtake him, he would look at me vengefully and run faster. Having increased his speed for some time, he would get out of breath and slow down. When I reached him, he would again give me that look and run faster. What kind of pleasure he derived from this was difficult to say, but he certainly raised my anxiety level.

One day, at Nehru Park, I had the misfortune of finding not one but two such fellows. They were running together and the moment I got near them, they sped up.

What was irritating was that they kept looking back and would speed up seeing me getting closer. This went on till we reached a point in the park where the path went up a rather sharp gradient of about fifty metres. As I was approaching that gradient, both these fellows who were running slowly, looked at me and instead of speeding up, gave me a piece of advice.

"*Aage pahaad hai. Jor se jaana hai* (There is a hill ahead, you have to increase your speed)," one of them said.

They were concerned that I may not be able to run up that gradient unless I increased my speed. Having said that, both of them sprinted up the gradient. I ran slowly and reached the top, where I found one of them lying on the ground and the other, bending down with his mouth open and breathing heavily.

They did not even have the strength of will to look at me. I also had no intention of engaging in any conversation with them or discussing the merits and demerits of that great piece of advice given by them. Such fellows definitely spoil that great feeling one has while running in peace.

One fine Sunday morning, I got up, fresh and happy. It was late October and the weather in Delhi was at its best. There was just a slight hint of chill and I set out for Lodhi Gardens for my run. Usually, I walked from my house on Shahjahan Road to the cemetery and then took the Amrita Shergill Marg up to the gardens.

Once I enter the garden, I start my run. That morning, I had a lovely walk up to the garden and then completed my four rounds of run around it. There were none of those runners who sped up on seeing you, making my run all the more pleasant. I passed small groups of very pleasant people, walking and smiling.

In all, it was a perfect way to start the day. After that bracing run, my endorphins had been released in abundance, giving me that heady feel-good feeling and with that, I left the garden and started walking back to my house. As I approached the cemetery, I saw something that made me stop.

By the cemetery wall, there was a makeshift florist's shop. It had not opened for business, but flowers of all varieties had been kept on the ground. There was a big bunch of liliums close to the wall. I saw a huge langur sitting on the wall, right above those flowers. He was holding a stick of lilium and slowly peeling off the petals and throwing them down.

The shopkeeper, who possibly had been woken up from his deep slumber by the invading langur, was holding a brick in one hand and had his gaze fixed on the monkey, watching his every move. The moment the monkey finished destroying one lilium, he would come down to pick up another. The man with the brick was just standing helpless. At this stage, I thought to intervene.

"*Kya hua*?" I whispered behind the man.

I admit it was an irrelevant and kind of idiotic question to ask at that point of time. On hearing a voice from behind, the man jumped up, startled and turned around. Seeing me with my short grey hair and my face, richly endowed with melanin, he possibly thought that a larger langur had approached him from behind. He let out a shriek, "Eeeeeii!"

Along with the shriek, he moved the brick up and was about to hit me with it, when I jumped back. Fortunately for me, my instinctive jump took me backwards and he could have a proper look at me, which made him realise that I was not a monkey after all. He turned around with a disgusted look and focussed on the continuing threat, which was taking a serious turn.

The monkey on the wall had alighted again and picked a few more sticks of lilium. The man just stood there, totally confused, seeing his inventory getting depleted by each move of the langur.

I left the place, quite shaken by this turn of events. I had to walk along the cemetery wall for a good distance and there was a lurking fear of more langurs to be encountered.

***